The Right to Be Lazy

and Other Essays

First Warbler Classics Edition 2023

First published in Paris 1883 and in Chicago in 1907 by Charles Kerr and Co.

Translation, Notes, and Biographical Timeline © 2023 Ulrich Baer

ISBN 978-1-959891-52-9 (paperback)
ISBN 978-1-959891-53-6 (e-book)

warblerpress.com

The Right to Be Lazy

and Other Essays

PAUL LAFARGUE

Newly Translated and Edited by Ulrich Baer

CONTENTS

PREFACE

In 1849, Mr. Thiers, at a session of the commission on pri-
mary education, said: "I wish to make the influence of the clergy
all-powerful because I count upon it to propagate that good philosophy which teaches man that he is here on earth to suffer, and
not that other philosophy which on the contrary says to man:
'Enjoy Yourself!'"[1] Mr. Thiers was expressing the ethics of the
bourgeois class, whose cruel selfishness and narrow-minded
intelligence he embodied.

When the bourgeoisie was still struggling against the nobility
backed by the clergy, they advocated free thought and atheism;
but once triumphant, they changed their tune and manner and
today use religion to support their economic and political control
and power. In the fifteenth and sixteenth centuries, they happily
adopted the pagan tradition and glorified the flesh and its passions, which Christianity had condemned. In our days, gorged
with goods and pleasures, they reject the teachings of their own
thinkers like Rabelais and Diderot, and preach abstinence to the
wage-workers.[2] Capitalist morality, a pitiful parody on Christian

---

1   [Adolphe Thiers (1797–1877), French politician, historian, Prime
Minister for two terms in 1836 and 1840, and President from 1871–1873. All
notes in brackets added by this volume's editor.]
2   [François Rabelais (born between 1483–1494, died 1533), French
Renaissance author, physician, and humanist known for writing satires;
Denis Diderot (1713–1784), French Enlightenment philosopher known as
co-founder and chief editor of the *Encyclopédie*.]

morality, detests as anathema the flesh of the worker; its ideal is to reduce the producer to the smallest number of needs, to suppress his joys and his passions and to condemn him to play the part of a machine churning out work without respite and without thanks.

The revolutionary socialists must take up again the battle fought by the philosophers and pamphleteers of the bourgeoisie. They must launch an attack on the ethics and the social theories of capitalism; they must demolish in the heads of the class which they call to action the prejudices sown in them by the ruling class; they must proclaim in the faces of the hypocritical moralizers of all persuasions that the earth shall cease to be the vale of tears for the worker and that in the communist society of the future, which we shall establish "peaceably if we may, forcibly if we must," the passions of men will be given free rein, for "they are all by nature good, and there is nothing to prevent but their misuse and their excesses." These passions will not be avoided except by their mutual counter-balancing and by the harmonious development of the human organism, for as Dr. Beddoe says, "only when a race reaches the maximum state of its physical development does it arrive at its highest point of energy and morality."[3] This was also the opinion of the great naturalist Charles Darwin.[4]

This refutation of the *"Right to Work"* which I am republishing with some additional notes appeared in the weekly *L'Égalité*, 1880, second series.

P. L.
Sainte-Pélagie Prison, 1883.

---

3   Dr. John Beddoe (1826–1911), English ethnologist, cited in *Memoirs Read Before the Anthropological Society 3* (1870); Charles Darwin (1809–1882), English naturalist, *The Descent of Man, and Selection in Relation to Sex* (1871).
4   René Descartes (1596–1650), French philosopher, *The Passions of the Soul* (1649).

THE RIGHT TO BE LAZY

Chapter 1

A DISASTROUS DOGMA

Let us be lazy in all things
just not lazy in loving and drinking
just not lazy in being lazy.
—Lessing[1]

A STRANGE DELUSION HAS SEIZED THE WORKING CLASSES OF the nations where capitalist civilization holds its sway. This delusion carries in its wake the individual and social woes which for two centuries have tortured sad humanity. This delusion is the love of work, the moribund passion for work, pushed to the point of exhaustion of the vital forces of the individual and his offspring. Instead of opposing this mental aberration, the priests, economists and moralists have cast a sacred halo over work. Blind and thick-headed men, they have wished to be wiser than their God; weak and contemptible men, they have wished to rehabilitate what their God had cursed. I, who do not profess to be a Christian, an economist or a moralist, I appeal against

---

1   [Gotthold Ephraim Lessing (1729–1781), German philosopher and author known especially for advocating religious tolerance.]

their judgement and for that of their God; from the preaching of their religious, economic or free-thinking morality to the horrific consequences of work in capitalist society.

In capitalist society work is the cause of all intellectual degeneracy, of all organic deformity. Compare the thoroughbred horses surrounded by a retinue of servants in Count Rothschild's stables with the lumbering farm horses of Normandy that plow the earth, cart the manure, and haul the crops. Look at the noble savage whom the missionaries of trade and the traders of religion have not yet corrupted with Christianity, syphilis and the dogma of work, and then look at our miserable slaves of machines.[2]

---

2   European explorers frequently pause in wonder before the physical beauty and the proud bearing of the people of primitive populations, not soiled by what explorer Eduard Poeppig calls "the poisonous breath of civilization." Speaking of the aborigines of the Oceanic Islands, Lord George Campbell writes: "There is not a people in the world which strikes one more favorably at first sight. Their smooth skin of a light copper tint, their hair golden and curly, their beautiful and happy faces. In a word, their whole person formed a new and splendid specimen of the human species; their physical appearance gave the impression of a race superior to ours." The civilized men of ancient Rome, namely Caesar and Tacitus, regarded with the same admiration the Germans of the communist tribes that invaded the Roman empire. Following Tacitus, Salvian, the priest of the fifth century who was called the *Master of the Bishops*, held up the barbarians as an example to civilized Christians: "We are immodest before the barbarians, who are more chaste than we. Even more so: the barbarians are wounded by our lack of modesty; the Goths do not permit debauchees of their own nation to remain among them; alone in the midst of them, by the sad privilege of their nationality and their name, the Romans have the right to be impure. [Pederasty was then the height of the fashion among both pagans and Christians.] The oppressed fly to the barbarians to seek humanity and shelter" (*De Gubernatione Dei* [On the Government of God]).—The old civilization and rising Christianity corrupted the barbarians of the ancient world, as the old Christianity and modern capitalist civilization are corrupting the savages of the new world.

Mr. Frédérick Le Play, whose talent for observation must be recognized, even if we reject his sociological conclusions, as they are tainted with philanthropic and Christian pretension, says in his book *The European Workers* (1885): "The propensity of the Bashkirs for laziness (the Bashkirs are semi-nomadic shepherds of the Asiatic slope of the Ural mountains); the leisure of nomadic life, the habit of meditation which this engenders in the best

When, in our civilized Europe, we wish to find a trace of the native beauty of man, we must go seek it in the nations where economic prejudices have not yet uprooted the hatred of work. Spain, which—regrettably!—is in the process of degenerating, may still boast of possessing fewer factories than we have prisons and army barracks. But the artist rejoices in his admiration of the hardy Andalusian, brown as his native chestnuts, straight and flexible as a steel rod; and the heart leaps at hearing the beggar, superbly draped in his ragged *capa*, addressing on equal terms the noblemen of Osuna as *"amigo."* For the Spaniard, in whom the primitive animal has not yet atrophied, work is the worst form of slavery.[3] During their epoch of greatness, the Greeks also had only contempt for work: their slaves alone were permitted to labor while the free man knew only exercises for body and mind. That was the era of men like Aristotle, Phidias, and Aristophanes; it was the time when a handful of heroes at Marathon crushed the hordes of Asia, soon to be subdued by Alexander. The philosophers of antiquity taught contempt for work, that degradation of the free man, while the poets sang of idleness, that gift from the Gods:

O Meliboee, deus nobis haec otia fecit.
O Melibous, a god wrought for us this leisure.[4]

Jesus, in his sermon on the Mount, preaches idleness:

Consider the lilies of the field, how they grow; they toil not,

---

endowed individuals—all this often gives them a distinction of manner and a refinement of intelligence and judgement that is rarely to be observed on the same social level in a more developed civilization…What is most repugnant to them is agricultural labor: they will do anything rather than accept the trade of a farmer." Agriculture is in fact the first example of servile labor in the history of man. According to biblical tradition, the first criminal, Cain, is a farmer.

3   The Spanish proverb says: *Descansar es salud* ("Rest is healthful").
4   [Virgil, *Bucolica* (1, 6).]

neither do they spin: yet I say unto you, that even Solomon in all his glory was not arrayed like one of these.[5]

Jehovah, the bearded and forbidding god, gave his worshipers the supreme example of ideal laziness; after six days of work, he rests for all eternity.

On the other hand, what are the races for which work is an organic necessity? The people of Auvergne; the Scotch, those Auvergnians of the British Isles; the Galicians, those Auvergnians of Spain; the Pomeranians, those Auvergnians of Germany; the Chinese, those Auvergnians of Asia.[6] In our society, which are the classes that love work for work's sake? The small farmers hunched over their fields and the little shopkeepers crouched in their shops, burrowing like moles in subterranean passages and never standing up to take a good and leisurely look at nature.

And even the proletariat, the great class comprising all the producers of civilized nations, the class which in freeing itself will free humanity from servile labor and will transform the human animal into a free being—this very proletariat, betraying its instincts and failing to recognize its historic mission, has let itself be perverted by the dogma of work. For that, its punishment has been harsh and terrible. All individual and social miseries arise from its passion for work.

---

5   [Matthew, 6:28–29.]
6   [The Auvergnians are inhabitants of the Auvergne region of France who are considered diligent and parsimonious.]

Chapter 2

BLESSINGS OF WORK

In 1770 in London, an anonymous pamphlet appeared with the title: "An Essay on Trade and Commerce." At the time it created a bit of a stir. The author, a great philanthropist, was indignant that

> the factory workers of England had taken into their head the fixed idea that in their quality of Englishmen all the individuals composing it have by birthright the privilege of being freer and more independent than the laborers of any other country in Europe. This idea may have its usefulness for soldiers, since it incites their courage, but the less the factory workers are imbued with it the better for themselves and the state. Laborers ought never to look on themselves as independent of their superiors. It is extremely danger-ous to encourage such notions in a commercial state like ours, where perhaps seven-eighths of the population own little or no property. The cure will not be complete until our working poor are content to work six days for the same sum which they now earn in four.[1]

Thus, nearly a century before French Prime Minister François

---

1   [Cited in Karl Marx, *Capital* (originally published 1867; Oxford University Press, 2008), vol. 1, "The Work Day."]

Guizot, work was openly preached in London as a way to curb the noble passions of man.[2]

The more my people work, the less vices they will have," wrote Napoleon on May 5th, 1807, from Osterode. "I am the authority [...] and I should be disposed to order that on Sunday after the hour of service, the shops be opened and the laborers return to their work.

To root out laziness and curb the sentiments of pride and independence which arise from it, the author of the "Essay on Trade" proposed to imprison the poor in "ideal workhouses," which should become "houses of terror where they should work fourteen hours a day in such a way that subtracting mealtime there should remain twelve full and complete hours of work."[3]

Twelve hours of work a day, that is the ideal of the philanthropists and moralists of the eighteenth century. How have we outdone this extreme state! Modern factories have become ideal houses of correction in which the toiling masses are imprisoned and where not only the men but also women and children are condemned to compulsory work for twelve or fourteen hours each day.[4] And to think that the sons of the heroes of the Terror have allowed themselves to be degraded by the religion of work,

---

2   [François Guizot (1787–1874), historian and French prime minister from 1847–1848.]

3   [Cited in Marx, *Capital* (op. cit).]

4   At the first Charitable Congress held at Brussels in 1857, one of the richest manufacturers of the town of Marquette, near Lille, Mr. Scrive, declared with the noble satisfaction of a duty well performed to the applause of the members: "We have introduced certain methods of diversion for the children. We teach them to sing during their work, also to count while working: That distracts them and makes them accept bravely *those twelve hours of labor which are necessary to procure their means of existence.*"—Twelve hours of labor, and what kind of labor, imposed on children less than twelve years of age! The materialists will always regret that there is no hell in which to confine these Christians, these humanists, these executioners of childhood!

to the point of accepting, starting in 1848 as a victory for the revolution, the law limiting factory work to twelve hours. They proclaim the *right to work* as a revolutionary principle. Shame on the French proletariat! Only slaves would have been capable of such baseness. Twenty years of capitalist civilization would have been needed to let a Greek of antiquity conceive of such vileness.

And if the miseries of compulsory work and the tortures of hunger have descended upon the proletariat in greater number than the locusts of the Bible, it is because the proletariat itself invited them.

This work, which in June 1848 the laborers demanded with weapons at the ready, they themselves have imposed on their families; they have delivered up to the titans of industry their wives and children. With their own hands they have demolished their domestic hearths; with their own hands they have dried up the milk of their wives. The unhappy women expecting and then nursing their infants have been forced to go into the mines and factories to bend their backs and exhaust their nerves. With their own hands they have smashed the life and the vigor of their children.—Shame on the proletarians! Where are those convivial matrons told of in our fables and our old tales, bold and frank of speech and never opposed to taking a draught from a bottle?[5] Where are those spirited young women, always on the move, always cooking, always singing, always spreading life and engendering life's joy, giving painless birth to healthy and strapping little ones?...Today we have factory girls and women, drooping flowers with pale faces, murky blood, irritable bowels, languid limbs...They have never known the pleasure of a healthful passion, nor would they be capable of recounting merrily how they lost themselves in love!—And the children? Twelve hours of work for children! What misery! But not all the Jules Simons

5   [Bacchus, Roman god of wine and viniculture.]

of the Academy of Moral and Political Science, not all the Jesuit Germinys, could have invented a vice more degrading to the intelligence of the children, more corrupting of their instincts, more destructive of their organism than labor in the blighted atmosphere of the capitalist factory.[6]

Our epoch has been called the century of work; in truth it is the century of pain, misery and corruption.

And yet all of the bourgeois philosophers and economists, from the painfully confused August Comte to the laughably lucid Leroy-Beaulieu, and the men of bourgeois literature, from the quackishly romantic Victor Hugo to the artlessly grotesque Paul de Kock, have intoned nauseating songs in honor of the god Progress, the eldest son of Work.[7] Listen to them and you would think that happiness was soon to reign on earth, and that we can already feel it coming. They turned their attention on past centuries where they sifted through its dust and its feudal miseries to bring back somber images that contrast to the delights of our present times.—How they have worn us out, these sated and satisfied people, until yesterday still part of the retinue of the nobility, today servile writers for the bourgeoisie with fat salaries; didn't they make us weary with descriptions of peasants, as invented by La Bruyère?[8] Well, here is the brilliant picture of proletarian delights in the year of capitalist progress 1840, created by one of their own men, Dr. Villermé. He was a member of the Institute and the same who in 1848 was a member of that society of learned men (Thiers, Cousin, Passy, the academician Blanqui, belonged to it), which spread among the masses the

---

6   [Jules Simon (1814–1896), French politician and philosopher.]
7   [August Comte (1798–1857), French philosopher and mathematician; Pierre Leroy-Beaulieu (1843–1916), French economist; Victor Hugo (1802–1885), French literary author and politician; Paul de Kock (1793–1871), French novelist.]
8   [Jean de La Bruyère (1645–1696), philosopher and moralist known for his satirical writings.]

platitudes of bourgeois economics and morality.[9]

Dr. Villermé speaks of the manufacturing region of Alsace—the Alsace of Kestner and Dollfus, those flowers of philanthropy and industrial republicanism. But before the doctor paints before us a complete picture of proletarian miseries, let us listen to how an Alsatian manufacturer, Mr. Th. Mieg, of the company of Dollfus, Mieg & Co., describes the situation of the craftsmen under the old commercial system:

> Fifty years ago (in 1813, when modern machine industry was just arising), all the workers in Mulhouse were children of the land, inhabiting the town and the surrounding villages, and almost all owning a house and often a small field.[10]

This was the golden age of the laborer. But at that time Alsatian industry did not deluge the world with its cottons, nor make millionaires out of its Dollfus' and Koechlins. But twenty-five years later, when Villermé visited Alsace, the modern Minotaur, in the form of the capitalist workshop, had conquered the countryside; in its insatiable hunger for human labor it had dragged the workers from their homes, the better to wring them and press out the labor which they contained. By thousands the workers flocked together at the signal of the steam whistle.

Villermé writes:

> A great number, five thousand out of seventeen thousand, were obliged by high rents to lodge in neighboring villages.

9   [Frédéric Passy (1822–1912), economist and politician who advocated for improving working conditions; Jérôme-Adolphe Blanqui (1798–1854), economist and elder brother of revolutionary Louis-Auguste Blanqui (1805–1881).]

10   Speech delivered before the International Society of Practical Studies in Social Economics, at Paris in May 1863, and published in the journal *Économiste Français* of the same period.

Some of them lived over two hours walking distance from
the factory where they worked.

At Mulhouse in Dornach, work began at five o'clock in the
morning and ended at eight o'clock in the evening, summer
and winter [...]. It was a sight to watch them arrive each morning into the city and depart each evening. Among them were
a multitude of pale, skinny women, often walking bare-foot
through the mud, and who for lack of umbrellas when it rained
or snowed wore their aprons or skirts pulled up over their heads
to protect face and neck. There was a still greater number of
young children, no less dirty and haggard, covered with rags,
greasy from the machine oil which drips on them while they
work. They were better protected from the rain because their
clothes shed water; but unlike the women just mentioned, they
do not carry a basket with their day's provisions, but hold in
their hands or hid under their apron as best they might, the
morsel of bread which must serve them as food until time for
them to return home.

Thus to the strain of an insufferably long day—at least
fifteen hours—are added for these wretches the constant
and onerous journeys to and from work. Consequently
they reach home overwhelmed by the need of sleep, and
the next day they rise before they are completely rested in
order to reach the factory by the opening time.

Now, consider the holes in which were packed those who
lodge in town:

I saw at Mulhouse, Dornach, and in neighboring houses
some of those miserable lodgings where two families slept
each in its corner on straw thrown on the floor and kept
in its place by two planks...This wretchedness among

the laborers of the cotton industry in the department of Haut-Rhin is so extreme that it produces the sad result, that while in the families of the manufacturers, merchants, factory traders or factory superintendents, half of the children reach their twenty-first year, this same half has died before the age of two in the families of weavers and cotton spinners.

Speaking of the labor in the sweatshops, Villermé adds:

It is not a work, a task, it is a torture and it is inflicted on children of six to eight years. [...] It is this long torture day after day which wastes away the laborers in the cotton spinning factories.

And as to the length of the work-day Villermé observes that the convicts in prisons work but ten hours, the slaves in the West Indies work but nine hours on average, while there existed in France, which had made its Revolution in 1789, and proclaimed the pompous *Rights of Man*, factories where a day's shift lasts sixteen hours, out of which the workers were allowed only an hour and a half for meals.[11]

Oh, what an abject miscarriage of the revolutionary principles of the bourgeoisie! Oh, what cruel gifts from its god Progress! The philanthropists hail as benefactors of humanity those who, in order to become rich while doing nothing, give work to the

---

11   Louis-René Villermé, *Data of the Physical and Moral State of Workers in Factories of Cotton, Wool and Silk* (1840). It is not because Dollfus, Koechlin and other Alsatian manufacturers were republicans, patriots and protestant philanthropists that they treated their laborers in this way, for Blanqui, the academician, Reybaud, the prototype of Jerôme Paturot [a fictional character in a novel by Louis Reybaud], and Jules Simon have observed the same amenities for the working class among the very catholic and monarchical manufacturers of the cities of Lille and Lyons. These are capitalist virtues which harmonize perfectly with all political and religious convictions.

poor. It would be better to spread the plague and poison the wells than to erect a capitalist factory in the midst of a rural population. Introduce factory work, and farewell to joy, health and liberty; farewell to all that makes life beautiful and worth living.[12]

And the economists do not tire of repeating to the laborers: "Work, to increase collective wealth!" And nevertheless an economist, Destutt de Tracy, responds: "It is in poor nations that people are comfortable, in rich nations they are ordinarily poor." [13] His disciple Cherbuliez continues:

The laborers themselves, in participating in the accumulation of productive capital, contribute to the event which sooner or later must deprive them of a part of their wages.[14]

But numbed and stupefied by their own howling, the economists answer: Work, always work, to create your prosperity! And in the name of Christian meekness a priest of the Anglican Church, the Rev. Mr. Townsend, intones: Work, work, night and day; by working you increase your misery and your misery releases us from imposing work on you by force of law. The legal imposition of work "gives too much trouble, requires too much violence and causes too much turmoil. Hunger, on the contrary,

---

12 The native people of the warrior tribes of Brazil kill their invalids and old people; they show their affection for them by putting an end to a life which is no longer enlivened by combats, feasts and dances. All primitive peoples have given these proofs of affection to their relatives: the Massageteans of the Caspian Sea (mentioned by Herodotus), as well as the Wends people of Germany and the Celts of Gaul. In the churches of Sweden even lately they preserved clubs called family clubs which served to deliver parents from the sorrows of old age. How degenerate are the modern proletarians to accept with patience the terrible miseries of factory labor!

13 [Antoine-Louis-Claude, Comte de Destutt de Tracy (1754–1836), economist and philosopher. The citation is from Marx, *Capital* (op. cit.) vol. 23.]

14 [Antoine-Èlisée Cherbuliez (1791–1869), Swiss writer.]

is not only a pressure which is peaceful, silent and incessant, but as it is the most natural motive for work and industry, it also provokes the most powerful efforts."[15]

Work, work, proletarians, to increase social wealth and your individual poverty; work, work, in order that becoming poorer, you may have more reason to work and become miserable. Such is the inexorable law of capitalist production.

Since they lend their ear to the deceptive speeches of the economists, the proletarians have given themselves up body and soul to the vice of work and precipitate the whole of society into these industrial crises of over-production which convulse the social organism. Then because there is a surplus of goods and a dearth of purchasers, the workshops are closed and hunger scourges the working people with its whip of a thousand lashes. The proletarians, brutalized by the dogma of work, not understanding that the over-work which they have inflicted upon themselves during the time of pretended prosperity is the cause of their present misery, do not run to the granaries of wheat and cry: "We are hungry, we wish to eat!...True, we have not a red cent, but beggars as we are, it is we, nevertheless, who harvested the wheat and gathered the grapes." They do not besiege the warehouses of Bonnet, in Jujurieux, the inventor of industrial convents, and cry out: "Mr. Bonnet, here are your working women, silk workers, spinners, weavers. They are shivering pitifully under their patched cotton dresses, yet it is they who have spun and woven the silk robes of the fashionable women of all Christianity. The poor creatures working thirteen hours a day, had no time to think of how they look. Now, they are out of work and have time to rustle in the silks they have made. Ever since they lost their milk teeth they have devoted themselves to your fortune and have lived in abstinence. Now they are at leisure and wish to enjoy a little of the

---

15   [Joseph Townsend (1739–1816), English theologian and sociologist. The citation is from Marx, *Capital*.]

fruits of their labor. Come, Mr. Bonnet, give them your silks, Mr. Harmel will furnish his muslins, Mr. Pouyer-Quertier his calicos, Mr. Pinet his boots for their dear little, cold and damp feet...Clad from top to toe and gleeful, they will be a delight to look at. Come, no evasions—you are a friend of humanity, are you not, and a Christian into the bargain? Put at the disposal of your working girls the fortune they have built up for you out of their own flesh.—You are a friend of business? Get your goods into circulation; here are consumers ready at hand, give them unlimited credit. You are regularly compelled to give such credit to merchants whom you do not know from Adam or Eve and who have given you nothing, not even a glass of water. Your working women will pay the debt the best they can. If at maturity they let their notes lead to protest and break their promises, you can declare them bankrupt and demand that they pay you in prayers: they will send you to paradise better than your black-gowned priests steeped in tobacco."[16]

Instead of taking advantage of periods of crisis, for a general distribution of their products and a universal holiday, the workers dying of hunger go and beat their heads against the factory gates. With pale faces and emaciated bodies, they assail the manufacturers pitiful speeches: "Dear Mr. Chagot, good Mr. Schneider, give us work! It is not hunger but the passion for work which torments us!" And these wretches, who have scarcely the strength to stand upright, sell twelve and fourteen hours of work twice as cheap as when they had bread on the table. And the humanist industrialists use unemployment to manufacture at lower cost.

If industrial crises follow periods of overwork as inevitably as night follows day, bringing after them forced unemployment and inescapable poverty, they also lead to inevitable bankruptcy. So

16   [Claude-Joseph Bonnet (1786–1867), silk manufacturer; built a factory with housing in Jujurieux.]

long as the manufacturer has credit he gives free rein to the rage for work. He borrows, and borrows again, to furnish raw material to his laborers, and goes on producing without considering that the market is becoming satiated and that if his goods don't happen to be sold, his debt notes will still come due. At his wits' end, he implores and throws himself at the feet of the bankers, offering his blood and honor. "A little gold would be quite preferable," answers Mr. Rothschild. "You have 20,000 pairs of hose in your warehouse; they are worth 20 cents. I will take them at 4 cents." The banker gets possession of the goods and sells them at 6 cents or 8 cents, and pockets the shiny coin for which he owes nothing to anybody. But the factory owner has been granted this short delay to fall even harder. At last the crash comes and the warehouses burst with products. Then so much merchandise is thrown out of the window that you cannot imagine how it came in by the door. Hundreds of millions are required to figure the value of the goods that are destroyed; in the last century they were burned or thrown into the water.[17]

But before reaching this decision, the manufacturers travel the world in search of markets for the goods that are piling up. They force their government to annex the Congo, to conquer Tonkin, to smash the Chinese Wall with cannon shots to make an outlet for their cotton goods. In previous centuries it was a duel to the death between France and England as to which should have the exclusive privilege of selling to America and the Indies. Thousands of young and vigorous men reddened the seas with their blood during the colonial wars of the sixteenth, seventeenth and eighteenth centuries.

There is a surplus of capital as well as of goods. The bankers no longer know where to place it. Then they venture among the happy people who are still loafing in the sunshine smoking

---

17   At the Industrial Congress in Berlin on January 21, 1879, the losses in the iron industry of Germany during the last crisis were estimated at 586 million Francs ($109,056,000 at the time).

cigarettes and there they lay down railroads, erect factories and import the curse of work. And this exportation of French capital ends one fine morning in diplomatic complications. In Egypt, for example, France, England and Germany were on the point of tearing each other by the hair to decide which usurers shall be paid first. Or it ends with wars like that in Mexico where French soldiers are sent to play the part of constables to collect bad debts.[18]

These individual and social miseries, however great and innumerable they may be and however eternal they appear, will vanish like hyenas and jackals at the approach of the lion, when the proletariat shall say "I will." But to arrive at the realization of its strength the proletariat must trample underfoot the prejudices of Christian, economic and liberal-minded ethics. It must return to its natural instincts, it must proclaim the *Rights of Laziness*, a thousand times more noble and more sacred than the anemic *Rights of Man* concocted by the metaphysical attorneys of the bourgeois revolution. It must accustom itself to working but three hours a day, reserving the rest of the day and night for leisure and feasting.

Thus far my task has been easy; I have had but to describe real evils well known, alas, by all of us; but to convince the proletariat that the ethics inoculated into it is unnatural and that the unbridled work to which it has given itself up for the last hundred years is the most terrible scourge that has ever struck

---

18   Mr. Clemenceau's newspaper *La Justice* states on April 6, 1880, in its financial section: "We have heard this opinion expressed, that even without the Prussians the billions of the war of 1870 would have been equally *lost* for France, that is in the shape of loans periodically set up to balance the budgets of foreign countries; this is also our opinion." The loss of English capital on loans to South American republics is estimated at five billion dollars. The French laborers not only produced the five billion dollars paid to German Chancellor Bismarck, but they continued to pay interest on the war indemnity to Ollivier, Girardin, Bazaine and other holders of pension titles, who brought on the war and the defeat. Nevertheless, they still have one shred of consolation: these billions will not bring on a war of reprisal.

humanity, that work will become a mere condiment to the pleasures of idleness, a beneficial exercise to the human organism, a passion useful to the social organism only when wisely regulated and limited to a maximum of three hours a day—that is an arduous task beyond my strength. Only physiologists, hygienists and communist economists could undertake it. In the following pages I shall merely try to show that given the modern means of production and their unlimited reproductive power it is necessary to curb the extravagant passion of the laborers for work and to oblige them to consume the goods which they produce.

Chapter 3

THE CONSEQUENCES OF OVER-PRODUCTION

A Greek poet of Cicero's time, Antiparos[1], celebrated the invention of the water-mill (for grinding grain) as the liberation of slave women and the return to the Golden Age:

> Spare the arm which turns the mill, oh millers, and sleep peacefully! Let the rooster warn you in vain that day is breaking. The goddess Demeter[2] has commanded the work of the girls to be done by the Nymphs; and now they skip lightly over the wheels, so that the shaken axles revolve with the spokes, and pull around the load of the revolving stones. Let us live the life of our fathers, and let us rest from work and enjoy the gifts that the goddess has sent us![3]

Alas! The leisure which the pagan poet announced has not come. The blind, perverse and murderous passion for work transforms the liberating machine into an instrument for the enslavement of free men. Its productivity impoverishes them.

A good female worker produces with her needles only five loops a minute, while certain circular knitting machines make

---

1   [Antiparos (first century A.D.), Greek poet.]
2   [Demeter, Greek goddess of fertility. The citation is also found in Marx, *Capital*, vol. 1]
3   [Antiparos (first century A.D.), Greek poet.]

30,000 in the same time. Every minute of the machine is thus equivalent to a hundred hours of the working women's labor, or again, every minute of the machine's labor, gives the working women ten days of rest. What is true for the knitting industry is more or less true for all industries reconfigured by modern machinery. But what do we see? The more the machine is improved and the more quickly and more precisely it performs a human worker's labor, the worker, instead of extending his former rest times, redoubles his ardor, as if he wished to rival the machine. O, absurd and murderous competition!

That the competition of man and the machine might run unimpeded, the proletarians have revoked the wise laws that had restricted the labor of the artisans of the ancient guilds; they have abolished the holidays.[4] Are we to believe the tales told by lying economists that because the laborers at that time worked but five days out of seven that they lived on nothing but air and spring

---

4   Under the *Ancien Régime* (dating from the end of the French monarchy to the Revolution), the laws of the church guaranteed the laborer ninety rest days, fifty-two Sundays and thirty-eight holidays, during which he was strictly forbidden to work. This was the great crime of Catholicism, and thus the principal cause of the irreligion of the industrial and commercial bourgeoisie: under the Revolution, once it had put itself in the saddle, it abolished the holidays and replaced the week of seven days by that of ten, in order that the people might no longer have more than one rest day out of ten. It emancipated the laborers from the yoke of the church in order the subjugate them all the better under the yoke of work.

The hatred against the holidays does not appear until the modern industrial and commercial bourgeoisie takes definite form, between the fifteenth and sixteenth centuries. Henry IV (1589–1610) asked of the Pope that they be reduced. He refused because "one of the current heresies of the day is regarding feasts" (Letters of Cardinal d'Ossat). But in 1666 Péréfixe, Archbishop of Paris, suppressed seventeen of them in his diocese. Protestantism, which was the Christian religion adapted to the new industrial and commercial needs of the bourgeoisie, was less concerned with the people's rest. It dethroned the saints in heaven in order to abolish their feast days on earth.

Religious reform and philosophical free thought were but pretexts which permitted the Jesuit and rapacious bourgeoisie to pilfer the feast days of the people.

water? What nonsense! They had leisure to taste earthly pleasures, to make love and to frolic, to feast happily in honor of the
jovial god of idleness. Gloomy England, mired in Protestantism,
was then called *Merry England*. Rabelais, Quevedo, Cervantes,
and the unknown authors of the romances make our mouths
water with depictions of those monumental feasts with which
the men of that time regaled themselves between two battles
and two devastations, in which everything "went by the bar-
rel."[5] Jordaens and the Flemish School have captured these
feasts for us in their delightful pictures. Where, oh where, are
the sublime gargantuan bellies of those days; where are the sublime brains that can encompass all of human thought? We have
indeed grown puny and degenerate. Embalmed beef, potatoes,
doctored wine and Prussian schnapps, cleverly combined with
compulsory labor have weakened our bodies and narrowed our
minds. And the times when man constricts his stomach and
the machine enlarges its output are the very times when the
economists preach to us the Malthusian theory, the religion of
abstinence and the dogma of work?[6] Really it would be better to
pluck out their tongues and throw them to the dogs.

---

5   These gigantic feasts lasted for weeks. Don Rodrigo de Lara wins his bride
by expelling the Moors from old Calatrava, and the *Romancero* relates the
story:

> Las bodas fueron en Burgos
> Las tornabodas en Salas:
> En bodas y tornabodas
> Pasaron siete semanas
> Tantas vienen de las gentes
> Que no caben por las plazas…

("The wedding was at Bourges,/ the second wedding day at Salas:/ with
the wedding celebrations/ seven weeks were spent./ So many people came/ that
the town could not hold them…"). The men of these seven-weeks weddings
were the heroic soldiers of the wars of independence.
6   [Thomas Robert Malthus (1766–1834), English theologian and economist
whose theory claims that population growth is exponential while growth in
resources is not.]

Since the working class, with its simple good faith, allowed itself to be thus indoctrinated and with its innate energy blindly hurled itself into work and abstinence, the capitalist class has found itself condemned to laziness and forced enjoyment, to unproductiveness and over-consumption. But if the extra-work of the laborer bruises his body and tortures his nerves, it also yields plenty of grief for the capitalist.

The abstinence to which the productive class condemns itself obliges the bourgeoisie to devote themselves to the over-consumption of the products turned out so riotously by the laborers. At the beginning of capitalist production a century or two ago, the capitalist was a steady man of reasonable and peaceable habits: He contented himself with one wife or thereabouts, drank only when he was thirsty and ate only when he was hungry. He left to the lords and ladies of the court the noble virtues of debauchery. Today there is no son of the newly rich who does think it his duty to cultivate prostitution and the disease for which quicksilver is a remedy, as a way of justifying the toil imposed upon the workers in quicksilver mines. There is no capitalist today who does not stuff himself with quails filled with truffles and the choicest brands of wine in order to encourage the breeders of poultry and the vintners of Bordelais grapes. While keeping busy like this the body rapidly falls apart, the hair falls out, the gums recede, the body becomes deformed, the stomach protrudes abnormally, respiration becomes difficult, the motions become labored, the joints become stiff, the fingers knotted. Others, too feeble in body to endure the fatigues of debauchery, but blessed with the aptitude for balderdash, dry up their brains to produce political economy or juridical philosophy in thick soporific books that occupy the leisure time of typesetters and publishers.

The women of this fashionable world live a life of martyrdom. In trying on and showing off the fairytale outfits which the seamstresses kill themselves to construct, they slip from morning to night out of one gown and into another. For hours on end they surrender their hollow heads to the hair artisans who at all cost wish to placate their passion for piling up false chignons. Bound in their corsets, pinched in their tight boots, with a cleavage to make a coal-miner blush, they whirl around the whole night through at their charity balls in order to pick up a few cents for the poor. Oh you sanctified souls!

To fulfill its dual social function of non-producer and over-consumer, the bourgeoisie was not only obliged to violate its modest tastes, to lose its laborious habits of two centuries ago and to surrender themselves to limitless luxury, truffle-induced indigestion and syphilitic debauchery, but also to withdraw from productive labor an enormous mass of men in order to enlist them as fellow gluttons.

Here are a few figures to how colossal is this waste of productive forces. According to the census of 1861, the population of England and Wales comprised 20,066,244 persons, 9,776,259 male and 10,289,965 female. If we deduct those who are too old or too young to work, the unproductive women, boys and girls, and also the "ideological professions," such as government, police, clergy, administration, soldiers, army, prostitution, arts, science, etc., and also the people exclusively occupied with consuming the labor of others in the form of rental income, interest, dividends, etc....there remain a total of eight million individuals of both sexes and of every age, including all of the capitalists engaged in production, commerce, finance, etc. Out of these eight million, the figures are:

Agricultural laborers, including shepherds, servants and farmers' daughters living at home)	1,098,261
Factory Workers in cotton, wool, hemp, linen silk, knitting	642,607

Metal Workers (blast furnaces, rolling mills, etc.)	396,998
Domestics	1,208,648

If we add together the textile workers and the miners, we obtain the figures of 1,208,442; if to the former we add the metal workers, we have a total of 1,039,605 persons; that is to say, in each case a number below that of the modern domestic slaves. Behold the magnificent result of the capitalist exploitation of machines.[7]

To this class of domestics, the size of which indicates the stage attained by capitalist civilization, must still be added the enormous class of unfortunates devoted exclusively to satisfying the vain and expensive tastes of the rich classes: diamond cutters, lace makers, embroiderers, binders of luxurious books, seamstresses for high fashion, interior decorators of villas, etc.[8]

Once settled down into absolute laziness and demoralized by enforced enjoyment, the capitalist class in spite of the injury involved in its new kind of life, adapted itself to it. Soon it began to look upon any change with horror. The sight of the miserable conditions of life resignedly accepted by the working class and the sight of the organic degradation engendered by the depraved passion for work increased its aversion for all compulsory labor and all restrictions of its pleasures.

It is precisely at that time that, without accounting for the

---

7   Marx, *Capital* (op. cit.), III.

8   "The proportion in which the population of the country is employed as domestics in the service of the wealthy class indicates its progress in national wealth and civilization." (Robert Montgomery Martin, *Ireland before and after the Union*, 1818). Gambetta, who has denied that there was a social question ever since he ceased to be the poverty-stricken lawyer of the Café Procope, undoubtedly alluded to this ever-increasing domestic class when he announced the advent of new social strata.

demoralization which the capitalist class had imposed upon itself as a social duty, the proletarians took it into their heads to inflict work on the capitalists. In their naïveté, they took seriously the theories of work proclaimed by the economists and moralists, and girded up their loins to inflict them in practice upon the capitalists. The proletariat proclaimed the slogan: "He who does not work, neither shall he eat."[9] In 1831, Lyons rose up in protest for "bullets or work," and the federated laborers of March 1871 called their uprising *"The Revolution of Work."*

To these furious, barbaric and destructive outbreaks against all capitalist joy and laziness, the capitalists had no other answer than ferocious repression. But even if they were able to suppress these revolutionary explosions, they knew that even in these oceans of spilled blood the absurd idea of the proletariat to inflict work upon the idle and reputable classes had not been drowned, and it is to avert this misfortune that they surround themselves with guards, policemen, judges and jailors, supported in laborious unproductiveness. There is no more room for illusion as to the function of modern armies; they are permanently maintained only to suppress the "enemy within." Thus the forts of Paris and Lyons were not built to defend the city against foreign invaders but to crush it in case of revolt. And if an irrefutable example is needed to illustrate this, we refer to the army of Belgium, that paradise of capitalism. Its neutrality is guaranteed by the European powers, and nevertheless its army is one of the strongest in proportion to its population. The glorious battlefields of the brave Belgian army are the plains of the Borinage and of Charleroi. It is in the blood of the unarmed miners and workers that the Belgian officers temper their swords and win their epaulets. The nations of Europe have not national armies but mercenary armies. They protect the capitalists against the popular fury which would

---

9   [Aphorism from the *New Testament*, Second Epistle to the Thessalonians].

condemn them to ten hours of mining or spinning.

While compressing its own stomach the working class developed abnormally the stomach of the bourgeoisie and condemned it to over-consumption.

In order to alleviate this painful labor, the bourgeoisie has withdrawn from the working class a mass of men far superior to those still devoted to useful production and has condemned them in their turn to unproductiveness and over-consumption. But no matter how insatiable and voracious this army of useless mouths may be, it alone cannot consume all the goods which the workers, stupefied by the dogma of work, produce like madmen without thinking to consume them and without even considering whether there will be people to consume them.

Confronted with this double madness of the workers killing themselves with over-production and vegetating in abstinence, the great problem of capitalist production is no longer to find producers and to multiply their powers but to discover consumers, to excite their appetites and create in them artificial needs. Since the European workers, shivering with cold and hunger, refuse to wear the fabrics they weave, to drink the wines from the vineyards they tend, the poor manufacturers in their goodness of heart must scour the ends of the earth to find people to wear the clothes and drink the wines, which is why Europe exports every year goods amounting to billions of dollars to the four corners of the earth to people who have no need of them.[10] But the newly explored continents are no longer vast enough; untouched virgin lands are needed. European manufacturers

---

10   Two examples: The English government, to satisfy the peasants of India who in spite of the periodical famines devastating their country insist on cultivating poppies instead of rice or wheat, has been obliged to undertake bloody wars in order to force the Chinese Government to permit the import of Indian opium. The native inhabitants of Polynesia, in spite of the mortality resulting from these habits, are obliged to dress and get drunk according to English customs in order to consume the products of the Scotch distilleries and the Manchester cotton mills.

dream night and day of Africa, of a lake in the Sahara, of a rail-road to the Sudan. They anxiously follow the progress of the likes of Livingstone, Stanley, Du Chaillu, and Brazza; they listen open-mouthed to the marvelous tales of these brave travelers. What unknown wonders are contained in the so-called "dark continent!" Fields are sown with elephants' tusks, rivers of cocoa-nut oil are dotted with gold, millions of backsides, as bare as the faces of Dufaure and Girardin, are awaiting cotton goods to learn decency, and also bottles of liquor and bibles to get to know the virtues of civilization.[11]

But to no avail: the over-fed capitalist, the servant class greater in numbers than the productive class, the foreign and barbarous nations, gorged with European goods—nothing, nothing can melt away the mountains of products piled in heaps higher and mightier than the pyramids of Egypt. The productiveness of European laborers defies all consumption, all waste. The manufacturers have lost their bearings and know not which way to turn. They can no longer find the raw material to satisfy the disorderly, depraved passion of their laborers for work. In our wool factories dirty and half rotten rags are raveled out to produce a kind of fabric sold under the label of "renaissance," which lasts about as long as electoral promises made to voters. Instead of leaving the silk fiber in its natural simplicity and suppleness, in Lyons it is saturated with mineral salts, which increase its weight but also make it friable and far from durable. All our products are adulterated to aid in their sale and shorten their life. Our epoch will be called the "Age of Falsification" just

11   [David Livingstone (1813–1873), Scottish physician, politician, explorer, and an immensely popular figure in Victorian England; John Stanley (1841–1904), Welsh-American explorer and administrator who located Livingstone in Africa after he had lost touch with Europe for six years; Paul Du Chaillu (1881–1903), French-American explorer and zoologist; Pierre Savorgnan de Brazza (1852–1905), French-Italian explorer; Jules Dufaure (1798–1881), two-term French prime minister; Ernest Stanislas de Girardin (1802–1874), French politician.]

as the first epochs of humanity received the names of "The Stone Age" and "The Bronze Age" from their mode of production. Ignorant people accuse our pious manufacturers of fraud, while in reality they are motivated by the idea to furnish work to their laborers, who cannot resign themselves to living with their arms folded. The sole motive for these distortions is a humanitarian sentiment, but they yield splendid profits to the manufacturers who practice them, even if they are disastrous for the quality of the goods and even if they are an inexhaustible source of waste in human labor. They prove the astute philanthropy of the bourgeoisie and the horrible perversion of the workers, who in order to satisfy their vice for work oblige the manufacturers to stifle the cries of their conscience and to violate even the laws of honest business.

And yet, in spite of the over-production of goods, in spite of the adulterations in manufacturing, the workers suffocate the market in countless numbers imploring: Work! Work! Their excessive numbers ought to compel them to bridle their passion—instead it drives them to madness. If there is a even chance for work anywhere, they rush at it; then they demand twelve, fourteen hours to glut their appetite for work, and the next day they are again thrown out on the pavement with no more food to satisfy their vice. Year after year in all industries lockouts occur as regularly as the change of seasons. Physically murderous over-work is followed by absolute rest during two or four months, and then—no work, no food. Since the vice for work is diabolically rooted in the heart of the workers, since its demands stifle all the other instincts of nature, since the quantity of work required by society is necessarily limited by consumption and by the supply of raw materials, why devour in six months the work of a whole year? Why not distribute it uniformly over the twelve months and force every worker to content himself with six or five hours a day throughout the year instead of getting indigestion from twelve hours during six months? Once assured of their daily portion of work, the workers will no longer be jealous of each other, no longer fight to snatch away work from each other's hands and bread from each other's mouths. Then, not exhausted in body and mind, they will begin to practice the virtues of laziness.

Stupefied by their addictive vice, the workers have been unable to grasp this fact: that to have work for all it is necessary to ration it like water on a ship in distress. Yet certain manufacturers in the name of capitalist exploitation have long demanded a legal limitation of the work day. One of the greatest manufacturers of Alsace, Mr. Bourcart of Guebwiller, declared before the 1860 Commission on Professional Education:

> The twelve-hour work day is excessive and ought to be reduced to eleven, while work ought to be stopped at two o'clock on Saturday. I advise the adoption of this policy, although it may appear too costly at first sight. We have tried it in our factories for four years now and find ourselves the better for it, while the average production, far from having diminished, has increased.

In his study *Of Machines,* Mr. F. Passy quotes the following letter from a Belgian factory owner, Mr. Ottevaere:

> Our machines, although the same as those of the English spinning mills, do not produce what they ought to produce or what those same machines would produce in England, although the spinners there work two hours less each day. [...] We all work two whole hours too much. I am convinced that if we worked only eleven hours instead of thirteen we would be as productive and consequently produce more economically.

Mr. Leroy Beaulieu also confirms: "An important Belgian manufacturer has noted that the weeks with a holiday result in no less productivity than regular weeks."[12]

An aristocratic government has dared to do what a people, duped into their simplicity by the moralists, never dared. Despising the lofty moral and industrial considerations of the economists, who like the birds of ill omen croaked that to reduce by one hour the work in factories was to decree the ruin of English industry, the government of England has forbidden by a strictly enforced law to work more than ten hours a day—yet as before, England remains the first industrial nation of the world.

The great English experience is on record; the experience of certain intelligent capitalists is on record: They prove beyond a doubt that to increase human productivity it is necessary to reduce the hours of labor and add more paid holidays—and yet the French people are still not convinced. But if the miserable reduction of two work hours has increased English production by almost one-third in ten years, what dizzying advance would it mean for French production to legally limit the working day to three hours? Can the workers not understand that by over-working themselves they exhaust their own strength and that of their progeny; that they are used up and, long before their time, become incapable of any work at all; that consumed and stupefied by a single vice they are no longer human beings but human wrecks; that they kill within themselves all beautiful faculties to leave nothing alive and flourishing except the furious madness for work?

Like the parrots of Arcadia they rotely repeat the lesson of the economists: "Let us work, let us work to increase the national wealth." O, you idiots! It is because you work too much that industrial technology develops slowly. Stop braying and listen to an economist—it is no luminary but no other than Mr. L.

---

12   Paul Leroy-Beaulieu, *The Workers' Question in the 19th Century*, 1872.

Reybaud, whom we were fortunate to lose a few months ago:

> The revolution in modes of production is generally deter-
> mined by the conditions of manual labor. As long as
> manual labor provides its services at a low price, it is exces-
> sively used, while efforts are made to limit its use when it
> becomes more costly.[13]

To force the capitalists to improve their machines of wood
and iron it is necessary to raise wages and diminish the working hours of the machines of flesh and blood. You need proof?
They can be furnished by the hundreds. In spinning factories,
the automated "self-acting mule" was invented and deployed
in Manchester because the spinners refused to work such long
hours as before.

In the United States the machine is invading all branches
of agricultural production, from the production of butter to
the weeding of wheat fields. Why? Because the free and lazy
Americans would prefer a thousand deaths to the cattle-like
existence of the French peasant. Plowing, so painful and so crip-
pling to the worker in our glorious France, is in the American
West an agreeable open-air pastime which a worker practices
sitting upright while leisurely smoking his pipe.

---

13   Louis Reybau, *Le coton: son régime, ses problems [Cotton: Its Reign and its
Problems]* (Paris, 1863).

Chapter 4

NEW SONG TO NEW MUSIC

IF BY REDUCING THE WORKING HOURS NEW MECHANICAL forces will be won for social production, by obliging the workers to consume what they produce an immense army of workers will be gained as well. Once relieved from its function of sole universal consumer, the disburdened bourgeoisie will rush to dismiss its hordes of soldiers, civil employees, hair stylists, matchmakers, etc., which it has withdrawn from useful labor to assist in its wasteful lifestyle of endless consumption. This will flood the labor market to such a degree that an iron law will be required to put a limit on work since it will be impossible to find employment for that swarm of formerly unproductive people, more numerous than locusts. Then one must consider all those who had provided for the vain and expensive needs and tastes of these people. Once there are no more lackeys and generals to decorate, no more unattached or married prostitutes to be wrapped in lace, no more cannons to cast and no more palaces to build, draconian laws will be required to compel the men and women now employed in producing finery, lace, iron works, and buildings to take up rowing and other types of exercise to restore their well-being and improve the race. The moment we begin to consume European products at home instead of sending them to the devil, it will be necessary that the sailors, railroad workers and truck drivers sit down and learn to twirl their thumbs. The

happy Polynesians may then love as they like without fear of getting kicked by the civilized Venus and the sermons of European
moralists.

There is more. In order to find work for all the non-producers
of our present society, in order to allow industrial equipment
to go on developing indefinitely, the working class will be compelled, like the capitalist class, to do violence to their proclivity
for abstinence and to develop indefinitely their capacities for
consumption. Instead of eating an ounce or two of gristly meat
once a day, if they eat any at all, they will consume large, juicy
beefsteaks; instead of drinking a bit of bad wine, being more
catholic than the pope, they will drain deep goblets brimming
with Bordeaux and Burgundy not baptized by industry, and will
leave water to the beasts.

The proletarians have taken it into their heads to inflict upon
the capitalists ten hours of work at the forge and factory—that
is the great mistake and the cause of social strife and civil wars.
Work ought to be forbidden and not imposed. The Rothschilds
and other capitalists must be permitted to testify to the fact that
for their entire lifetime they have been complete slackers, and if
they swear they wish to continue to live as perfect loafers in spite
of the general mania for work, they should be registered as pen-
sioners and receive every morning at the city hall a five-dollar
gold piece as pocket money. Social discords will vanish. Bond
holders and capitalists will be the first to rally to the people's
party, once convinced that far from wishing them harm, its purpose is rather to relieve them of the labor of over-consumption
and waste with which they have been burdened since birth. As
for the capitalists who are incapable of proving their claim as
certified slackers, they will be allowed to follow their instincts:
there are plenty of revolting occupations in which to place them.
Dufaure would clean public bathrooms, Gallifet would gore

scabrous hogs and mangy horses.[1] The members of the amnesty commission, dispatched to the central prison at Poissy, will tag the oxen and the sheep to be slaughtered. The senators might play the part of undertakers and lackeys in funeral processions. As for the others, occupations could be found for them on a level with their intelligence. Lorgeril and Broglie could cork champagne bottles, but they would have to be muzzled so they wouldn't get intoxicated. Ferry, Freycinet and Tirard might be tasked with exterminating bugs and vermin in the departments of state and other public buildings.[2] It would be necessary, however, to store the public funds out of reach of the capitalists given their acquired habits.

But harsh and prolonged vengeance will be heaped upon the moralists who have perverted nature, the bigots, the charlatans, the hypocrites,

and other such sects of men who disguise themselves to deceive the world. For while they give the common people the impression that they are busy with nothing but contemplation, devotion, fasting and suppressing their sensuality and that their fragile humanity is just barely kept alive while doing so—it is certainly so very different that, on the contrary, God knows what cheer they make; *et Curios simulant, sed Bacchanalia vivunt.* [They simulate to live like (the paragon of virtue) Curius but live like (the orgiastic) Bacchanals].[3] You may read it in great, fiery letters in their

1   [Gaston de Galliffet (1830–1909), general responsible for the massacre of French workers during the Paris Commune, the French revolutionary government that briefly seized power in 1871.]
2   [Hippolyte de Lorgeril (1811–1888), poet and politician; Jacques-Victor-Albert (1821–1901), historian and politician; Jules Ferry (1832–1893), minister and prime minister; Charles de Freycinet (1828–1923), engineer and politician; Pierre Tirard (1827–1893), politician and two-term prime minister.]
3   Juvenal [Roman poet, late first and early second century CE], *Satires* (written 100–127 A.D.).

red cheeks and bloated bellies, unless they perfume themselves with sulphur.[4]

During great public holidays, when instead of swallowing
dust as on the 15th of August and 14th of July under capitalism, the communists and collectivists eat, drink and dance to
their hearts' and bodies' content, the members of the Academy
of moral and political sciences, the priests with short robes or
cassocks of the economic, Catholic, Protestant, Jewish, positivist
and free-thinking church; the representatives of Malthusianism
and of Christian, altruistic, independent or dependent ethics,
clothed in yellow, shall be compelled to hold a candle until it
burns their fingers, and in sight of joyful women near tables
loaded with meats, fruits and flowers they shall starve and go
thirsty in sight of overflowing barrels. Four times a year with the
change of seasons they shall like the knife grinders' dogs be put
inside great treadmills and grind wind for ten hours. Lawyers
and legislators shall suffer the same punishment.

Under the regime of idleness, to kill the time which murders
us second by second, there will be perpetually running shows
and theater performances—a task perfectly suited to our bourgeois legislators. We shall organize them into traveling companies to visit fairs and villages and present legislative exhibitions.
Generals in riding boots, their breasts decorated with medals,
chains and the cross of the Legion of Honor shall roam the
streets to recruit the good people to the show. Gambetta and
his comrade Cassagnac shall be the doormen at these events.[5]
Cassagnac, in full dueling outfit, shall roll his eyes, twist his mus-
tache, spit fire and threaten every one with his father's pistol but

---

4   François Rabelais, *The Life of Gargantua and of Pantagruel: Pantagruel*,
Book II: Chapter XXXIV (originally published 1532). Translation by Sir
Thomas Urquhart of Cromarty and Peter Antony Motteux.
5   [Paul Granier de Cassagnac (1842–1904), politician famous for frequent
duels.]

drop into a hole as soon as they show him Lullier's portrait.[6] Gambetta will ramble on about foreign politics and little Greece which pulls the wool over his eyes and would set Europe on fire to pilfer Turkey; about great Russia which stultifies him with the mincemeat it promises to make of Prussia and who would happily see chaos reign in western Europe so as to feather its nest in the East and to strangle nihilism at home; on Mr. Bismarck who was kind enough to say something about the amnesty…Then he will strip bare his large belly smeared with the three national colors of red, white and blue, beat the signal to retreat and recount all the delicate roasted songbirds, truffles, and goblets of Margaux and Yquem that he downed to encourage agriculture and to keep the voters of Belleville in good spirits.

In the barracks the entertainment will open with the *Electoral Farce*.

In the presence of the voters with wooden heads and asses' ears, the bourgeois candidates, dressed as clowns, will dance the dance of political liberties, wiping themselves fore and aft with their electoral programs stuffed with promises, and talking with tears in their eyes of the miseries of the people and with brass in their voices of the glories of France. Then the heads of the voters will bray solidly in chorus, Hee haw! Hee haw!

Then the curtain rises on the main play: *The Theft of the Nation's Goods*.

Capitalist France, an enormous woman, hairy-faced and bald-headed, fat, flabby, puffy and pale, with sunken eyes, sleepy and yawning, is reclining on a velvet couch. At her feet Industrial Capitalism, a gigantic iron organism with an ape-like mask is mechanically devouring men, women and children, whose mournful and heart-rending cries fill the air. The bank, with a weasel's snout, a hyena's body and harpy-hands, is nimbly

---

6   [Charles Lullier (1838–1891), marine officer and elected member of the Paris commune.]

filching coins out of its pocket. Hordes of miserable, emaciated proletarians in rags, escorted by gendarmes with drawn sabers, pursued by furies lashing them with whips of hunger, are depositing at the feet of capitalist France heaps of merchandise, casks of wine, and entire sacks of gold and wheat. Amédée Langlois, member of the International, his undergarment in one hand and the testament of Proudhon in the other, with the ledger of the national budget between his teeth, is encamped at the head of the defenders of national property and is mounting guard.[7] As soon as the workers, beaten with gun barrels and pricked with bayonets, have laid down their burdens, they are driven away and the gates are opened to the manufacturers, merchants and bankers. They hurl themselves pell-mell upon the heap, devouring cotton fabric, sacks of wheat, ingots of gold, and emptying casks of wine. Finally, they have had their fill and sink down, filthy and disgusting objects in their dirt and vomit...Then thunder bursts forth, the earth shakes and opens—and Historic Destiny appears. With her iron foot she crushes the heads of the capitalists who are hiccupping, staggering, falling, unable to flee. With her immense hand she overthrows capitalist France, astonished and sweating with fear.

If, uprooting from its heart the vice which dominates it and degrades its nature, the working class were to arise in its terrible strength, not to demand the *Rights of Man* which are but the rights of capitalist exploitation, not to demand the *Right to Work* which is but the right to misery, but to forge an iron-clad law forbidding any man to work more than three hours a day, then the earth, the old earth, would tremble with joy and sense a new universe stirring inside...But how should we ask a proletariat corrupted by capitalist ethics to start a mighty resolution!

Like Christ, the doleful personification of the slaves of

---

7   [Amédée Jérôme Langlois (1819–1902), marine officer and member of the Paris commune; Pierre-Joseph Proudhon (1809–1865), economist and sociologist know as a founder of anarchism.]

antiquity, the men, women and children of the proletariat have been climbing painfully for a century up the hard Calvary of pain: For a century forced labor has broken their bones, bruised their flesh, tormented their nerves; for a century hunger has ravaged their guts and put hallucinations in their brains! O Laziness, have pity on our long misery! O Laziness, mother of the arts and noble virtues, be the balm of human anxieties!

Chapter 5

APPENDIX

OUR MORALISTS ARE QUITE MODEST PEOPLE. ALTHOUGH THEY invented the dogma of work, they still have doubts of its efficacy in calming the soul, rejoicing the spirit, and maintaining the proper functioning of the loins and other organs. They wish to try its workings on the populace, *in anima vili* on a subject of little value, before turning it against the capitalists, to excuse and authorize whose vices is their particular mission.

But, you, dime-a-dozen philosophers, why thus pound your brains to work out an ethics the practice of which you dare not recommend to your masters? Do you wish to see your dogma of work, of which you are so proud, scoffed at and dishonored? Let us examine the history of ancient peoples and the writings of their philosophers and law givers.

"I could not affirm," says the father of history, Herodotus, "whether the Greeks derived from the Egyptians the contempt which they have for work, because the Thracians, the Scythians, the Persians, the Lydians and nearly all foreign peoples also look down as the lowest of citizens all craftsmen and even their children. All the Greeks, particularly the Lacedaemonians, have been raised on this principle."[1]

"At Athens the citizens were veritable nobles who had to

---

1   Herodotus [Greek historian, 484–425 BCE], *Histories*, Book II.

concern themselves but with the defense and the administration of the community, like the savage warriors from whom
they descended. Since they must thus have all their time free to
watch over the interests of the republic, with their mental and
bodily strength, they placed all labor upon the slaves. Likewise at
Lacedaemon, even the women were not allowed to spin or weave
so as not to detract from their nobility."[2]

The Romans recognized but two noble and free professions:
agriculture and arms. All the citizens by right lived at the expense
of the state but could not be constrained to provide for their
living by any of the "sordid arts" (which is what they called the
trades), which by right belonged to the slaves. The elder Brutus,
to incite the people, accused the tyrannical Tarquin the Proud of
the specific outrage of having converted free citizens into artisans and masons.[3]

The ancient philosophers had their disagreements about the
origin of ideas but they agreed when it came to the abhorrence
of work.

"Nature," writes Plato in his social utopia, his model *Republic*,
"nature has made no shoemaker nor smith. Such occupations
degrade the people who exercise them. Vile mercenaries, name-
less wretches, who are by their very condition excluded from
political rights. As for the merchants accustomed to lying and
deceiving, they will be allowed in the city only as a necessary evil.
The citizen who shall have degraded himself by the commerce of
the shop shall be prosecuted for this offense. If he is convicted,
he shall be condemned to a year in prison; the punishment shall
be doubled for each repeated offense."[4]

In his *Economics*, Xenophon writes:

---

2   Édouard Biot, *The Abolition of Ancient Slavery in the West*, 1840.
3   Livy [Roman historian, 59 BCE–AD 17], *History of Rome*, Book I.
4   [Plato, *Republic*, book V. These sentences are not found as such in Plato's
works but combine statements found in Plato's *The Republic* and *The Laws*.]

The people who give themselves up to manual labor are never promoted to public offices, and with good reason. The greater part of them, condemned to be seated the whole day long, some even to endure the heat of the fire continually, cannot fail to be changed in body, and it is almost inevitable that the mind be affected.

"What honorable thing can come out of a shop?" asks Cicero. "What can commerce produce in the way of honor? Everything called a shop is unworthy of an honorable man. Merchants can gain no profit without lying, and what is more shameful than falsehood? Again, we must regard as something base and vile the trade of those who sell their toil and industry, for whoever gives his labor for money sells himself and puts himself in the rank of slaves."[5]

Proletarians, brutalized by the dogma of work, do you hear the voice of these philosophers, which has been concealed from you with jealous care?—A citizen who sells his labor for money degrades himself to the rank of slaves; he commits a crime which deserves years of imprisonment.

Christian hypocrisy and capitalist utilitarianism had not yet perverted these philosophers of the ancient republics. Since they spoke to free men, they expressed their thought freely. Plato and Aristotle, these intellectual giants, beside whom our latter-day philosophers are but tiny dwarves even when stretching up on tip-toe, wished for the citizens of their ideal republics to live in the greatest possible leisure, for as Xenophon observed: "Work takes up all the time and with it one has no leisure for the republic and one's friends." According to Plutarch, Lycurgus, "wisest of men," deserved the great admiration of posterity because he granted leisure to the citizens of Sparta by

---

5   Cicero, *On Duties*, Book I, 42.

forbidding them any trade whatever.[6]

But, our moralists of Christianity and capitalism reply: "These thinkers and philosophers praised the institution of slavery."[7]—Perfectly true, but could it have been otherwise, granted the economic and political conditions of their epoch? War was the normal state of ancient societies; free man was obliged to devote his time to discussing the affairs of state and watching over its defense. The trades were then too primitive and coarse for those practicing them to exercise their birthright of soldier and citizen; thus the philosophers and law-givers, if they wished to have warriors and citizens in their heroic republics, were obliged to tolerate slaves.—But don't the moralists and economists of capitalism praise the system of wage labor, modern-day slavery? And to what kind of men does the capitalist slavery give leisure?—To people like Rothschild, Schneider, and Madame Boucicaut, useless and harmful freeloaders and slaves of their vices and of their domestic servants.[8]

"The prejudice of slavery dominated the minds of Pythagoras and Aristotle,"—this has been written disdainfully; and yet Aristotle foresaw: "For if each of the instruments were able to perform its function on command or by anticipation, as they assert those of Daedalus did, or the tripods of Hephaestus (which the poet says 'of their own accord came to the gods' gathering'), so that shuttles would weave themselves and picks play the lyre, master craftsmen would no longer have a need for subordinates,

---

6   Plato, *Republic*: book V, and *Laws*: book III; Aristotle, *Politics*: books II and III; Xenophon, *Economics*, books IV and VI; Plutarch, *The Life of Lycurgus*.
7   [Lafargue here references Frédéric Bastiat (1801–1850), economist; Félix-Antoine-Philibert Dupanloup (1802–1878), bishop of Orléans, and Paul Leroy-Beaulieu (1843–1916), economist.]
8   [Gustave Samuel James de Rothschild (1829–1911), French banker; Joseph Eugène Schneider (1805–1875), French industrialist and politician; Marguerite Boucicaut (1816–1887), co-owner of the first department store in Paris, "Bon Marché."]

or masters for slaves."[9]

Aristotle's dream has become reality for us. Our machines, with breath of fire, with limbs of unbending steel, with wonderful and inexhaustible fertility, accomplish by themselves and eager for more commands their sacred labor. And nevertheless the genius of the great philosophers of capitalism remains dominated by the prejudice of the wage system, the worst type of slavery. They do not yet understand that the machine is the savior of humanity, the god who shall redeem man from the "sordid arts" and from salaried work, the god who shall grant him leisure and liberty.

---

9   [Aristotle, *Politics*, Book 1, chapter 4, translated by Carnes Lord (Chicago, 2013).]

THE WOMAN QUESTION[1]

BOURGEOIS MAN HAS THOUGHT AND STILL THINKS THAT women ought to remain at home and devote their activities to supervising and managing the household, caring for her husband, and producing and feeding children. Even Xenophon, at the time when the bourgeoisie was newly born and was taking its shape in ancient society, traced the main outlines of this ideal of woman. But if over the course of centuries this ideal seemed reasonable because it corresponded to the economic conditions of the time, today it indicates nothing any longer but the last remnants of an ideology, since these conditions have ceased to exist.

The domestication of woman presupposes that she fulfills in the household numerous functions which absorb all her energy; now, the most important and most burdensome of these domestic labors—the spinning of wool and linen, the cutting and tailoring of clothes, laundry work, daily baking, etc.—are carried out by capitalist industry. It furthermore presupposes that man

---

1   [First published in French as "La question de la femme," in *Édition de L'Œuvre Nouvelle* (Paris, 1904). Translation by Charles Kerr, in *The Right To Be Lazy and Other Studies* (originally published in 1904), modified and annotated by Ulrich Baer. For discussions of Lafargue's evolving position on and engagement with the role of women, see especially Leslie Derfler, *Paul Lafargue and the Flowering of French Socialism, 1882–1911* (Cambridge, MA: Harvard University Press, 1998), and Karen Offen, *Debating the Woman Question in the French Third Republic, 1870–1920* (Cambridge: Cambridge University Press, 2017). Notes in brackets by the editor.]

contributes to the family's capital and its material needs with his wealth and ongoing income. Among the comfortable bourgeoisie, marriage is as much an association of capital as a union of individuals, and often the capital contributed by the wife exceeds that of the husband,[2] while in the lower middle-class the fathers'

---

2   Dowry payments have played an important role in the history of woman: at the beginning of the patriarchal period the husband buys her from her father, who has to refund her purchase price if for any cause whatever the husband repudiates her and sends her back to her family; later this purchase price is returned to him and constitutes her dowry, which her relatives are accustomed to double. From the moment when the wife moves into her husband's house with a dowry, she ceases to be a slave whom he may dismiss, sell and kill. The dowry, which in Rome and Athens became a legal charge upon the property of the husband, was in case of her repudiation or divorce, to be restored to her before any restitutions to creditors. "No pleasure is derived from the riches which a woman brings into the household," says a fragment of Euripides, "they only serve to render divorce difficult." The comic authors ridiculed the husbands, who in fear of a legal suit over the dowry, became dependent on the wife. A character in Plautus says to a husband who is speaking out against his wife, "You accepted the money of her dowry, you sold your authority—now she reigns." The wealthy Roman matrons carried their insolence to such a point that they did not trust the management of their dowry to their husbands but handed it over to the stewards, who sometimes fulfilled with them another service, as reported by the evil-tongued Martial.

Adultery on the part of the wife involved a legal divorce and the restitution of the dowry, but rather than reach this painful extreme state, the husbands preferred to close their eyes to the foibles of their wives. In Rome and Athens, the law had to strike at married women in order to recall them to their marital dignity; in China a certain number of bamboo strokes were applied to the soles of their feet. Since the penalties were not sufficient to encourage the husbands to repudiate their adulterous wives, the law, in order to prop up masculine virtue, permitted those who denounced their wife's infidelity to retain a part of the dowry: there were also men who married only in anticipation of the wife's adultery. Roman women evaded the law by having themselves enrolled in the censor's book on the list of prostitutes, to whom they did not belong. The number of matrons registered in this way grew so much that the Roman Senate under Tiberius passed a decree forbidding "women who had a patrician for a grandfather, husband or father to traffic in their bodies." (Tacitus, *Annals* II., 85.) Adultery on the part of the wife in patrician society of antiquity, as well as in the aristocratic society of the eighteenth century, had become so general that it had effectively become a social custom. It was looked upon lightly as a corrective and common dimension of marriage.

incomes have fallen so low that sons as well as daughters are forced to earn their living in business, railroad administration, banks, teaching, civil service, etc. It often happens that a young, newly married wife continues to work outside the home in order to contribute resources to the household, since the husband's income is not sufficient to cover expenses.

The daughters and wives of the lower middle-class, as well as those of the working class, thus enter into competition with their father, brothers and husband. This economic antagonism, which the bourgeoisie had prevented by confining the wife to the family home, is becoming more wide-spread and intensifies in proportion to the rise of capitalist production. It invades the liberal professions, such as medicine, law, literature, journalism, the sciences, etc., where man had kept for himself a monopoly which he imagined was to be eternal. The workers, as is always the case, have been the first to draw the logical consequences of the participation of women in social production. They have replaced the ideal of the artisan—the wife as nothing but a housekeeper—with a new ideal: woman as an ally in their economic and political struggles for the increase of wages and the emancipation of labor.

The bourgeoisie has not yet reached the understanding that its ideal of what a woman ought to be is already long since outdated and must be reconfigured to reflect the new social conditions. Nevertheless, since the first half of the nineteenth century the ladies of the bourgeoisie have begun to protest against their relegation to an inferior position in the family, which is so much more intolerable once their dowry placed them on equal economic footing with the husband. They rebelled against the domestic slavery and parsimonious life to which they were condemned, as well as against the deprivation of intellectual and material enjoyments which was imposed upon them. The bolder ones among these women went so far as to demand free love and to ally themselves with the utopian sects which preached the emancipation of woman.[3] Our philosophers and moralists were naïve enough to believe that they could stop the feminist movement by opposing to it the sacred interest of the family, which they declared could not survive without subjecting women to household work (the sewing on of shirt buttons, the mending of socks, etc.). Her duty was to devote herself to these obscure and thankless chores so that man might freely deploy and display his brilliant and superior faculties. These same philosophers, who lectured the rebellious ladies on the cult of the family, sang the praises of capitalist industry, which, by tearing the wife away from the hearth and her child's cradle and condemning women to the forced labor of the factory, destroys the working-class family.

The ladies of the bourgeoisie laughed at the partly imbecile and partly ethical sermons of these solemn philosopher-quacks; they stayed the course and reached the goal they set for themselves. Like the patrician ladies of Roman antiquity and the aristocrats of the eighteenth century, they delegated the cares of housekeeping and child-rearing to paid servants, so that they might devote themselves wholly to their appearance to become the most luxuriously arrayed dolls in the capitalist world, who could then also conduct business. The daughters and wives of the American plutocracy have reached the extreme limits of this sort of emancipation; they are transforming their fathers and husbands into accumulators of millions, which they squander madly. Since being fashionable does not exhaust the entire activity of the ladies of capitalism, they find ways of amusing themselves in breaking the marriage contract in order to assert their independence and improve the race. *The Communist Manifesto*

---

3   The Saint Simon manifesto of 1830 announced that the religion of Saint Simon had come "to put an end to that shameful traffic, legal prostitution, which under the name of marriage often blesses the monstrous union of self-surrender and egoism, of light and of ignorance, of youth and decrepitude."

explains that the countless divorce suits in which adultery is alleged are indisputable proof of the respect inspired in both middle-class men and women by the sacred bonds of marriage which the licentious socialists talk of loosening.

When the daughters and wives of the lower middle-class, once forced to earn their living and contribute to the resources of the family, began to invade stores, offices, civil service and the liberal professions, the bourgeoisie was gripped with anxiety for their already severely curtailed means of existence, which feminine competition would reduce still further. The intellectuals who took up the defense of men were careful not to repeat the ethical sermons which had miscarried so pathetically in the case of the wealthy bourgeois ladies. Instead they appealed to science and demonstrated with high-minded and presumably irrefutable arguments that women cannot leave their role of housekeepers without violating the laws of nature and of history. They proved to their complete satisfaction that woman is an inferior being, incapable of receiving a higher education and lacking the combination of attention, energy and agility required of the professions where she entered into competition with man. Her brain, less voluminous, less heavy and less complex than that of man, they claimed, is a "child's brain." Her less developed muscles lack the strength for attack and for resistance; the bones of her forearm, her pelvis, her femur, and in fact her entire skeletal, muscular and nervous system do not permit her to undertake more than routine household tasks. Nature designed her in a way that makes her fit to be nothing but the servant of man, just as the vengeful God of the Jews and Christians condemned the race of Ham with the mark for slavery.

History contributed its startling confirmation of these ultra-scientific truths. The philosophers and historians affirmed that it teaches us that always and everywhere the wife, subordinate to the man, had been shut up in the house and in separate woman's dwellings; if such had been her lot in the past, such was to be her destiny in the future—thus proclaimed Auguste Comte, the profoundest of middle-class philosophers. Cesare Lombroso, that illustrious comedian, did him one better: he seriously declared that social statistics proved the inferiority of woman, since the number of female criminals is lower than that of male criminals.[4] While he plunged into these figures, he might have added that the statistics of insanity demonstrate the same inferiority. Thus we see that ethics, anatomy, physiology, social statistics and history riveted forever upon woman the chains of domestic servitude.

2.

Bachofen, Morgan and many anthropologists have revised the opinion of historians and philosophers about the role played by woman in the past.[5] They have shown that everywhere the paternal family, which subordinated woman to man, had been preceded by the maternal family, which assigned women to the first position. The Greek language registers these two conditions: while the Spartans, among whom matriarchal customs persisted, still continued to call her *he despoinia*, "the mistress of the house" and the "sovereign," the other Greeks gave to the wife the name *he damar*, "the subdued, the vanquished." In the *Odyssey*'s description of Nausicaa, we find that she is *parthenos admes*, the "girl not subdued," that is to say without a husband, without a master. The modern expression "yoke of virginity"

<hr>

4   [Auguste Comte (1798–1857), French philosopher, founder of positivism, and considered the first philosopher of science; Cesare Lombroso (1835–1907; Italian criminologist, phrenologist and physician.]
5   [Johann Jacob Bachofen (1815–1887), Swiss anthropologist and sociologist, famous for this theory of matriarchy; Lewis Henry Morgan (1818–1881), American anthropologist and social theorist.]

preserves that ancient notion.

Hesiod, in opposition to Homer, who recounts only patriarchal customs, preserves precious recollections of the matriarchal family; he tells us that when it existed, "man, even if he were a hundred years old, lived with his prudent mother and was fed in her house like a full-grown child.[6] It was not the woman who then had the "child's brain" but the man; everything seems in fact to prove that her intelligence was the first to develop. This intellectual superiority caused her to be deified before man in the original religions of Egypt, the regions of and near India, Asia and Greece, and led to the first inventions of the arts and trades, except metal working, being attributed to goddesses and not to gods. The Muses, originally three in number, were in Greece held in higher esteem than even Apollo as goddesses of poetry, music and dance. Isis, "mother of corn ears and lady of bread," and Demeter, lawgiver, had taught the Egyptians and Greeks the cultivation of barley and wheat and made them renounce their cannibal habits. The woman appeared to pre-patriarchal man, like the Germans whom Tacitus knew, as having within herself "a certain uncanny and prophetic sense."[7] Her prudence and foresight gave her this divine character. Must we conclude that this intellectual superiority, which became manifest when economic conditions were rudimentary, is a natural phenomenon?

It may be asserted in any case that the vitality of woman is superior to that of man. The life insurance companies of the United States, England and Holland, which do not base their calculations upon scientific fairy tales spun by intellectuals but upon mortality tables, pay woman an annuity below that which they assign to man, because her probabilities of death are lower. Here for example is the annuity paid for a capital of $1,000 by

---

6   [Hesiod, *Works and Days*, trans. Hugh Evelyn-White (New York, 1914), V: 129–130.]

7   "*Aliquid sanctum et providum*," in Tacitus, *Germania*, trans. W. Peterson and M. Hutton, (Cambridge, 1914), 8.

American and Dutch companies:[8]

Age	New York Men	New York Women	Holland Men	Holland Women
50 years	$76.47	$69.57	$76.80	$73.60
60 years	97.24	88.03	98.50	93.50
70 years	134.31	122.48	142.0	136.70
80 years	183.95	168.00	222.70	211.70

It may be objected that man, leading a more active life, is more subject to accidents, diseases, and other causes of death, and that consequently the prolonged life of woman does not prove the higher vitality of her organism, but the advantages of a life less subject to accident.

The answer to this objection is found in the statistics of the various nations. There is in no country a perfect equilibrium between the number of women and that of men; for 1,000 men there are in Belgium 1,005 women, in France 1,014, in England 1,062, in Scotland 1,071 and in Norway 1,091. Nevertheless, in these countries with the feminine preponderance there is an excess of masculine births: of the whole of Western Europe for every 1000 girls there are born from 1,040 to 1,060 boys. If, in spite of this excess of masculine births, more girls survive, it is because the greater mortality of the boys restores the balance in favor of the girls; and this higher mortality cannot be explained by the life of man being more subject to accident, since it is observed at an early age, notably during the first two years. All the diseases of childhood, with the exception of diphtheria and

---

8   The French companies make no differences between the sexes because they pay very small annuities. *La Génerale*, the most important one in France, offers for $1,000 at the age of 50 years an annuity of $64.20: at 60 years $80.80; at 70 years $118.50; at 80 years $134.70. Thus it realizes immense profits: its shares which in 1819 were worth 780 francs each were quoted last January at 31,300 francs.

whooping cough, are noticeably more fatal among boys than among girls, from zero to five years the male sex is particularly frail; at all ages, except between ten and fifteen years, the male mortality is in excess of the female.

The superior vitality of the female sex is also noticeable in the greater ease with which the female body recovers from illness. Mr. Iribe, superintendent of the sanitarium of Hendaye, which receives Parisian children from three to fourteen years of age who are afflicted with anemia, incipient tuberculosis, scrofula and rickets, reports that at the time of their dismissal, at the end of six months, "the increase in weight, girth and chest development is incomparably higher in the girls than in the boys" while the increase in weight is double and often more.

The same statement has been made by other superintendents of sanitariums. (Bulletin Medical, No. 81 [1903].)

Woman undeniably possesses a greater vitality than man. Mr. Gustav Loisel has conducted research "as to whether this difference existed in embryonic life, and what may be its cause?" He has communicated the results of his inquiries to the Biological Society of Paris, which published them in its Bulletin of November 6, 1903.

Mr. Loisel availed himself of 792 weights and measurements made upon 72 fetuses at the Maternity Hospital of Paris by Mr. E. Legou[9]; from the following weights of the fetuses at three, four, five and six months he obtains the following figures:

	Males Grammes	Females Grammes	Differences Grammes
Total weight	1908.18	1708.11	200.07 in favor of males
Kidneys	16.87	17.19	0.32 – females

9   E. Legou, *Some Considerations on the Development of the Fetus* (Paris 1903).

	Males Grammes	Females Grammes	Differences Grammes
Suprarenal glands	5.15	6.43	1.28 – females
Liver	88.35	96.31	7.96 – females
Spleen	2.59	2.38	0.21 – males
Thymus	3.89	3.97	0.08 – females
Heart	10.97	12.60	1.63 – females
Lungs	47.29	44.62	2.67 – males
Brain	236.94	235.17	1.77 – males

"These figures thus show us," writes M. Loisel, "a preponderance in favor of the females as regards the kidneys, the suprarenal glands, the liver, the thymus and the heart: this predominance is the more noticeable since the total weight of the body is larger in the male than in the female."

If now we consider the relation between the total weight and the weight of the organs which are heaviest in the male, we find that the proportion is still in favor of the female:

	Proportion of Total Weight	
	Males	Females
Spleen	1 to 736	1 to 718
Lungs	1 to 40	1 to 38
Brain	1 to 8	1 to 7

The organs here examined, brain included, are thus absolutely or relatively heavier in the female fetus than in the male fetus.

Mr. Loisel has also conducted research into the proportion of the weights of the different organs to the total weight according to the age of the fetus. He has prepared a table, from which I take only the figures concerning the brain:

Age	Total Weight		Proportion of weight of brain to total weight	
	Males grammes	Males grammes	Males	Females
3 months	58.33	65.96	1/6.5	1/7
4 months	167.25	182.58	1/7.3	1/6.6
5 months	336.33	295.00	1/7.6	1/7.5
6 months	732.58	636.00	1/8.3	1/7.3

The weight of the male fetus, which is below that of the female fetus at three months when the sex has just been determined, increases more rapidly and the proportion between the total weight and the weight of the brain is always to the advantage of the females, starting with the fourth month.

"To sum up," says Mr. Loisel,

all the organs are heavier in the female fetus than in the male fetus up to about the fourth month. The predominance then passes over to the male, but only for the lungs and the genital organs, while the cardiac muscle always remains heavier in the female. The organs which are of real service to the individual during the embryonic life always remain more developed in the female sex.

If now we consider that the differences in favor of the females are especially in the liver, the heart, the suprarenal glands and the kidneys, we shall reach the conclusion that the greater vitality of the female organisms corresponds to their being better nourished and better purified.

3.

The superior organization possessed by woman at birth and that assures her throughout her life a much greater vitality, is probably required by the part she plays in the reproduction of the species, a part far more prolonged and exhausting than that of the man who, once fertilization has been accomplished, has no further tasks, while only then the true labor of woman begins during the long months of pregnancy and following birth. The women of savage tribes breastfeed their children for two years and more. It sometimes happens that the male pays dearly for his inutility; after union, the bees kill the males, and the male spider must hastily remove himself so that he may not be devoured by the larger and stronger female. Among the ancient Sumerians, at the annual feasts of the Babylonian female goddess Mylitta-Anaïtis, they sacrificed the handsome slave who had just united with the priestess who incarnated the Assyrian goddess.[10] This bloody religious ceremonial must have been a reproduction of an Amazonian custom.

The life of savagery and barbarism permits woman to develop her intellectual superiority of birth; each sex there has its special function, where the division of labor first appears. The man, whose muscular system is more developed, "fights, hunts, fishes and sits down," according to Australian aboriginals who considers everything else to fall under the sway of woman, whose role engages mental activity at an earlier stage. She is in charge of the communal house, which often shelters a clan of more than one hundred individuals; she prepares clothing from skins and other raw materials; she is responsible for cultivating the garden, the rearing of domestic animals and the manufacture of household utensils; she preserves, economizes, cooks and distributes the vegetable and animal provisions which are gathered throughout the year; and like the Valkyries of the Scandinavians and the Keres of the pre-Homeric Greeks, she accompanies the warrior

10   [Mylitta (also Mullissu), goddess known as the wife of Enlit, in the Mesopotamian pantheon 4th century BCE, and identified in Greek mythology with the goddess of love, Aphrodite.]

on the battle field, aids in the fray, revives him if he is wounded and cares for him.[11] Her assistance is so highly valued that, according to Tacitus, the barbarians who under the leadership of Civilis revolted against Emperor Vespasian were seized with pity for the Roman soldiers because their wives did not accompany them when they marched into battle. Plato who like the elite group initiated in the Eleusinian Mysteries was also more knowledgeable about ancient customs than generally supposed, lets women assist the warriors in battle in his *Republic*.[12]

These multiple and diverse functions, which forced woman to reflect, calculate, and think of tomorrow and to take a longer view of things, must necessarily have developed her intellectual faculties; thus the craniologists say that only a slight difference exists between the cranial capacity of the two sexes among native Black populations, Australians, and native Americans, while they find that it steadily increases among civilized people. Woman appears to the carefree savage who lacks foresight to be a form of providence; she is the prudent and prescient being who rules his destiny from birth to death. Man, who arranges his religions in accordance with the events and intellectual tasks of daily life, was thus obliged to begin by deifying woman. The pre-historic Greeks and Romans had placed their destinies under the control of goddesses, the Fates—the Moirai and the Parcae—whose name signifies in Latin "sparing," "economical," and in Greek designates the part which falls to each one in the distribution of food or of booty.

Once we relieve the rich and poetic Greek mythology of the symbolical, allegorical and mystical phrasings with which the philosophers and the poets of the classical epoch and the Alexandrine period have overloaded and complicated it, and

---

11 [Valkyries, female figures in Norse mythology who guide souls of the dead on their journey. Keres, female death-spirit figures in Greek mythology.]
12 [Eleusinian Mysteries, initiations in ancient Greece for the cult of the goddesses Demester and Persephone.]

which the German mythologists, slavishly copied by those of France and England, have developed into their own more perfect confusion, then we have the inestimable record of prehistoric customs that correspond to the contemporary customs which travelers and anthropologists now observe again among the savage and barbaric nations of Africa and the New World. Mythology thus furnishes us with information of the relative value of feminine and masculine intelligence among the Greeks, before they had entered upon the patriarchal period.

Jupiter, the "father of the gods," as Homer, Hesiod and Aeschylus call him, after having driven the feminine divinities from Olympus enthroned the patriarchy there, which for some generations had been established upon earth: The heaven of religion always reflects the customs on earth, just as the moon reflects the light of the sun. But Jupiter, who like every barbarian knew how to use his fists (*Iliad,* XV: 228) and boasted that he was the strongest of the gods who dominated the others and who kept next to his throne two servants, Force and Violence, always ready to obey his orders, was inadequately prepared by his intellectual dualities to replace woman in the government of the Olympian family. In order to supply the capacities which were lacking to him, Hesiod tells us that he married Metis, "the wisest among mortals and gods." The savage and the barbarian still devour their enemies' throbbing heart in order to literally incorporate their courage. Zeus similarly devoured Metis to assimilate her cunning, her prudence and her wisdom, for her name in Greek has these diverse meanings. All these qualities were considered as belonging to woman.

But the process of assimilation took some time, if we may judge from the devious farce played upon Jupiter by Prometheus. The latter killed and butchered an enormous ox, and placed in one pile the flesh which he covered with the skin upon which he deposited the entrails; in another pile he put the bare bones adroitly concealed under heaps of fat. "You have divided the parts very badly," said the father of gods and men. "Most worthy Jupiter, greatest of living gods, take the part that your wisdom counsels you to choose," replied the astute Prometheus. The ruler of the heavens, listening only to his gluttony, laid both hands upon the heap of fat amid the laughter of the Olympians; his wrath was terrible when he saw the bare bones (*Theogony*, 435 et seq.) Such a farce would hardly have been played in the Olympian heaven had it not been that on earth similar tests had been required to prove to the Father that his intellectual faculties did not allow him to take the place of the Mother in the leadership of the family and the management of its property.

The higher position in the family and society, which man conquered by brute force, while it compelled him to a mental activity to which he was little accustomed, at the same time put at his disposal ever-increasing opportunities for reflection and development. Woman, "subdued," as the Greek expression has it, shut up in the narrow circle of the family, the leadership of which had been taken from her, and having little or no contact with the outside world, saw on the contrary an almost complete reduction of the means of development which she had enjoyed, and to complete her subjection she was forbidden the intellectual culture which was given to man. If in spite of these fetters and these disadvantages, the disastrous effects of which cannot be exaggerated, the brain of woman continued to evolve, it was because woman's intelligence benefited from the progress achieved by the masculine brain. For one sex transmits to the other the qualities which it has acquired, just as the pullets of certain chicken varieties inherit the spurs which are very developed among the roosters, while in other varieties they transmit to the males their exaggerated crests. "It is indeed fortunate," writes Charles Darwin on this point, "that the law of the equal transmission of characters to both sexes prevails with mammals;

otherwise, it is probable that man would have become as superior in mental power to woman, as the peacock is in ornamental
plumage to the peahen."[13]

But defects as well as valuable qualities are transmitted from
one sex to the other: if woman has profited by the brain-growth
of man, he has in his turn been delayed in his development by
the slowing-down of the development of woman's brain, resulting from the reduction to the bare minimum of intellectual
activity to which he has condemned her. The breeders who seek
the choicest results are as careful to have irreproachable females
as males: amateur cockfighters attach as much importance to
the selection of the pullets as to the cocks and only allow those
which are armed with spurs and which have the fighting spirit to
reproduce. It may be said that humanity, since it emerged from
the communism of the clan to live under the system of private
property, has developed only be the efforts of one sex alone and
that its evolution has been delayed through the obstacles inter-
posed by the other sex. By systematically depriving woman of
material and intellectual means of development, man has turned
her into a force retarding human progress.

If we study and compare the different periods of savagery and
barbarism, we cannot but observe the continuous and remarkable progress made by the human mind, because women and
men, exercising freely their physical and mental faculties, contribute equally to the evolution of the species. This evolution
has slowed down ever since humanity entered into the period
of civilization and private property, because from that point on
women, constrained and confined in her development, could
not contribute to it as effectively. The sterile stagnation in which
China has endured for more than a thousand years can only
be attributed to the degradation of woman, which has gone to

---

13   Charles Darwin, *Descent of Man* (London and New York: Penguin, 2004),
VIII and XIX.

the point of the cruel mutilation of her feet that she may be imprisoned the more closely in the women's quarters. Europe also suffers from the degradation of woman, since in spite of the extraordinary material progress of the last two millennia and the increasing and no less extraordinary accumulation of scientific knowledge, the brain of modern, civilized man cannot be said to exceed in power and capacity that of the Greeks of the classic epoch, which extends from the seventh to the fourth century before the Christian era. It is certain that novelists like a Victor Hugo or an Émile Zola, or any university graduate or doctor has stored in his brain an abundance of positive and diverse ideas not possessed by Aeschylus, Anaxagoras, Protagoras, and Aristotle.[14] But that does not prove that his or his contemporaries' imagination and intelligence is richer, more varied and vaster than that of the generations of Ionia and Attica, who created that incomparable flourishing of science, philosophy, literature and art at which history marvels and who reveled in that subtle and paradoxical play of sophist philosophy, the likes of which has not been seen again. The sophists, including Protagoras, Gorgias, Socrates, Plato, etc., stated, discussed and solved the problems of the philosophy of life and mind and many others besides: yet the Hellenes of Asia Minor and of Greece had emerged from barbarism only a few centuries before. One can cite many reasons that explain this arrest in human development, but the principal one is the subjection of woman.

4.

Capitalist production, which assumes control of most of the

14 [Victor Hugo (1802–1885), French novelist and politician; Lafargue wrote a critical essay about his works; Émile Zola (1840–1902), French journalist and literary author; Aeschylus (525–456 BCE), Greek tragedian; Anaxagoras (5th century BCE), Greek philosopher; Protagoras (490–420 BCE), Greek philosopher; Aristotle (384–322 BCE), Greek philosopher.]

tasks to which woman had previously devoted herself in a middle-class house, has enlisted into its army of wage-workers in factories, shops, offices and schoolrooms the wives and daughters of the working class and of the small bourgeoisie in order to procure cheap labor. In its pressing need of intellectual skills, it has set aside the venerable and venerated axiom of masculine ethics that "reading, writing and counting ought to be the full extent of woman's knowledge" and instead made it necessary that girls just as boys receive at least rudimentary education in the sciences. The first step was taken; women could no longer be forbidden from entering the universities. They proved that the feminine brain, which the intellectuals had declared a "child's brain," was as capable as the masculine brain of being taught science. The abstract sciences (mathematics, geometry, mechanics, etc.), which were the first whose study had been accessible to woman, were also the first in which they could demonstrate their intellectual capacities. Women are now attacking the experimental sciences (physiology, physics, chemistry, applied mechanics, etc.), and in America and Europe there arise legions of women who march on a level with men in spite of the inferior conditions of physical and moral development in which they have lived since early childhood.

As Capitalism has not torn woman from the domestic hearth and cast her into social production in order to emancipate her but to exploit her more ferociously than man, so it has been careful not to overthrow the economic, legal, political and moral barriers which had been raised to imprison her in the marital home. Woman, exploited by capital, endures the miseries of the free worker and bears in addition her chains of the past. Her economic misery is aggravated; instead of being supported by her father or husband, to whose rule she continues to submit, she is obliged to earn her living. Under the pretext that she has fewer needs than man, her labor is paid less; and when her daily work in the workshop, the office or school is ended, her work in the household begins. Motherhood, the sacred task and the highest of social functions, becomes in capitalist society a cause of horrible economic and physiological misery. The social and economic condition of woman is a danger for the reproduction of the species.

But this crushing and pitiful condition spells the end of her servitude, which begins with the establishment of private property and which can end only with its abolition. Civilized humanity, under the pressure produced by mechanical modes of production, turns toward a society, based on common property, in which woman, delivered from the economic, legal and moral chains which bind her, may develop freely her physical and intellectual faculties, as in the time of the communism of the savages.

The so-called savages, to prohibit primitive promiscuity and effectively delimit the circle of permitted sexual relations, found no other means than to separate the sexes; there are reasons for believing that the women took the initiative in this separation, which the specialization of their functions consolidated and emphasized. This separation became socially established by religious ceremonies and secret languages that were specific to each gender and even by physical strife;[15] and after having taken the form of violent antagonism, it ended in the brutal subjugation of woman, which still persists although it progressively diminishes in proportion to the way the competition between the sexes spreads and intensifies in the economic sphere. But the modern antagonism will not end with the victory of one sex over the other, for it is one of the phenomena of the struggle of labor against capital, which will find its solution in the

---

15   A. W. Howitt (1830–1908; Australian anthropologist and naturalist), who observed among the Australians a species of sexual totemism, says that it often happens that the women and men of one clan fight when the animal that serves as the totem for one sex is killed by the other sex.

emancipation of the working class in which women as well as men are incorporated.

The means of production that tend to suppress the specialization of trades and functions and to replace muscular effort by mental aptitude and intellectual skills and that, the more they are perfected, enmesh and confound man and woman all the more in social labor, will prevent the return of the conditions which in savage and barbarous nations had maintained the separation of the sexes. Common property will put an end to the economic antagonism of civilization.

But if it is possible to catch a glimpse of the end of female servitude and of the antagonism of the sexes and to conceive for the human species an era of incomparable bodily and mental progress, achieved by women and men of high physical and mental sophistication, it is impossible to foresee the sexual relations between free and equal women and men who will be neither united nor divided by sordid material interests and the coarse ethics engendered by them. But if we may judge by the present and the past, men, in whom genetic passion is more violent and more persistent than in women (the same phenomenon is observed in males and females of the whole animal kingdom) will be forced to exhibit all of their physical and mental qualities to win over their beloved. Sexual selection, which, as Darwin has shown, fulfilled an important role in the development of the animal species and which, with rare exceptions, has ceased to play this part in the Indo-European races for about three thousand years, will again become one of the most active factors in perfecting the human race.

Motherhood and love will permit woman to reconquer the superior position that she occupied in primitive societies, the memory of which had been preserved by the legends and myths of the ancient religions.

THE BANKRUPTCY OF CAPITALISM

THE NINETEENTH CENTURY WAS THE CENTURY OF CAPITALISM. Capitalism filled that century to overflowing with its commerce, its industry, its manners, its fashions, its literature, its art, its science, its philosophy, its religion, its politics and its civil code, more universal than the laws imposed by Rome upon the nations of the ancient world. The capitalist movement, starting from England, the United States and France, has shaken the foundations of Europe and of the world. It has forced the old feudal monarchies of Austria and Germany and the barbaric despotism of Russia to put themselves in order; and more recently it has gone into the far East, into Japan, where it has overthrown the feudal system and implanted the industry and the politics of capitalism.

Capitalism has taken possession of our planet; its fleets knit together the continents which oceans had separated; its railroads, spanning mountains and deserts, furrow the earth; the electric wires, the nervous system of the globe, link all nations, and their palpitations reverberate in the great centers of population. Now for the first time there is a contemporaneous history of the world. Events in Australia, the Transvaal, and China become known in London, Paris, and New York at the moment they occur, just as if they happened in the outskirts of the city where the news is published.

Developed nations today live off the products of the entire

planet. Egypt, India, and Louisiana furnish the cotton, Australia the wool, Japan the silk, China the tea, Brazil the coffee, New Zealand and the United States the meat and grain. The capitalist carries in his stomach and wears on his back the spoils of the universe.

The study of natural phenomena has undergone an unprecedented and unheard-of development. New sciences, geology, chemistry, physics, etc., have appeared. The industrial deployment of the forces of nature and of the discoveries of science have become even more startling; some of the discoveries of geometry which the scientists of Alexandria made two thousand years old are put to use for the first time.

The goods supplied by industrial production can meet all existing demand and more. The mechanical application of the forces of nature has increased man's productive forces ten and even a hundredfold. A few hours' daily labor, furnished by the able-bodied members of the nation, would produce enough to satisfy the material and mental needs of the world's population.

But what has been the result of this colossal and wonderful development of science, industry and commerce in the nineteenth century? Has it made humanity stronger, healthier, happier? Has it given leisure to the workers? Has it brought comfort and contentment to the people?

Never has work been so prolonged, so exhausting, so damaging to man's body and so deadly to his intelligence. Never has the industrial labor that undermines health, shortens life and starves the intellect been imposed so sweepingly on such ever-growing masses of workers. The men, women and children of the proletariat are bent under the iron yoke of machine industry. Poverty is their reward when they work, starvation when they lose their jobs.

In former stages of society, famine appeared only when the earth refused her harvests. In capitalist society, famine moves into the homes of the working class when granaries and cellars burst with the fruits of the earth, and when the market is gorged with the products of industry.

All the toil, all the production, all the suffering of the working class has done nothing but increase its physical and mental destitution, to drag it from misery to misery.

Capitalism, controlling the means of production and directing the social and political life of a century of science and industry, has become bankrupt. The capitalists have not even proved competent, like the owners of chattel slaves, to guarantee to their worker the labor that is necessary to support their miserable livelihood; capitalism massacred them when they dared demand the right to work—a slave's right.[1]

The capitalist class has also made a failure of itself. It has taken hold of the wealth of social productions to enjoy it, and never was the ruling class more incapable of enjoyment. The newly rich, those who have built up their fortunes by accumulating what they filched from labor, live like strangers in the midst of luxury and priceless artworks, with which they surround themselves in a foolish display of vanity to pay homage to their millions.

The leading capitalists, the millionaires and billionaires, are sad, useless and destructive specimens of the human race. The mark of degeneracy is upon them. Their sickly offspring are old at birth. Their organs are sapped with diseases. Exquisite meats and wines weigh down their tables, but the stomach refuses to digest them; women expertly skilled in love spread a fragrance of youth and beauty in their rooms, but their senses are numb. They own palatial dwellings in enchanting sites, and they have no eyes, no feeling for jubilant nature with its eternal youth and change. Sated and disgusted with everything, they are followed everywhere by ennui as by their shadows. They yawn when they

---

1   I allude to the June Days uprising of 1848 in Paris, when the insurgents demanded the "Right to Work."

rise and when they go to bed; they yawn at their parties and at their orgies. They began yawning in their mother's womb.

The pessimism which, in the wake of capitalist property, made its appearance in ancient Greece six centuries before the birth of Christ, and which has since formed the foundation of the moral and religious philosophy of the capitalist class, became the leading characteristic of the philosophy of the second half of the nineteenth century. The pessimism of the ancient Greek poet Theognis sprang from the uncertainties and vicissitudes of life in the Greek cities, torn by perpetual wars between rich and poor; the pessimism of the capitalist is the bitter fruit of satiety, ennui and the impoverishment of the blood.[2]

The capitalist class is lapsing into its second childhood; its decrepitude appears in its literature, which now reverts to its point of departure. Romantic literature, the literary form proper to the capitalist class, which started out with the romantic Christian kind written by Chateaubriand, is returning to the same origin, after having passed through the historical novel and the novel of characters.[3] Capitalism, which in its virile and combative youth in the eighteenth century had wished to emancipate itself from Christianity, resigns itself in its old age to practices of the grossest superstition.

The capitalist class, bankrupt, old, useless and harmful, has finished its historic mission; it persists as ruling class only through its acquired momentum. The proletariat of the twentieth century will execute the decree of history by driving it from its position of social control. Then the stupendous work in science and industry accomplished by civilized humanity, at the price of such toil and suffering, will engender peace and happiness; then will this vale of tears be transformed into an earthly paradise.

---

2   [Theognis (6th century BCE), Greek lyric poet.]
3   [François-René Chateaubriand (1768–1848), writer, politician, diplomat, and historian of considerable influence in the first half of the 19th century.]

SIMPLE SOCIALIST TRUTHS[1]

WORKER. But if there were no masters, who would give me work?

SOCIALIST. That's a question I am often asked; let us examine it. In order to work, three things are required: a workshop, machines, and raw material.

W. Right.

S. Who builds the workshop?

W. Masons.

S. Who made the machines?

W. Engineers.

S. Who grew the cotton you weave, who sheared the wool your wife spins, who dug the mineral your son forges?

W. Farmers, shepherds, miners—workers like myself.

S. Consequently, you, your wife, and your son can only work because these various other workers have already supplied you with buildings, machinery, and raw material.

W. Indeed, that's true; I could not weave calico fabric without cotton and without a loom.

---

1   [First English translation published in *The Socialist*, September 1903. Translation modified by Ulrich Baer.]

S. Well then, it is not the capitalist or master who gives you work, but the mason, the engineer, the ploughman. Do you know how your master has procured all that is necessary for your work?

W. He bought it.

S. Who gave him the money?

W. How do I know? His father had left him a little; today he is a millionaire.

S. Has he earned his million by working his machines and weaving his cotton?

W. Not very likely; it is by making *us* work that he earned his million.

S. Then he has grown rich by loafing; that is the only way to make a fortune. Those who work get just enough to live on. But, tell me, if you and your fellow workers did not work, would not your master's machines rust, and his cotton be eaten by insects?

W. Everything in the workshop would go to wreck and ruin if we did not work.

S. Consequently, by working you are preserving the machines and raw material necessary for your labor.

W. That is true; I had never thought of that.

S. Does your master look after what goes on in his workshops and factory?

W. Not much; he makes a daily round to see us at our work, but he keeps his hands in his pockets for fear of dirtying them. In the spinning-mill, where my wife and daughter work, the masters are never seen, although there are four of them; still less so in the foundry, where my son works; the masters are never seen nor ever known; not even their shadow is seen since it is a Limited

Liability Company that owns the works. Suppose you and I had five hundred francs saved up, we could buy a share, and become one of the masters, without ever having put, or without putting, a foot in the place.

S. Who, then, directs and manages the work in this place belonging to the shareholding masters, and in your own shop of one master, given that the masters are never there, or so rarely that it doesn't count?

W. Managers and foremen.

S. But if it is workers who have built the workshop, made the machines, and produced the raw materials; if it is workers who keep the machines going, and managers and foremen who direct the work, what does the master do, then?

W. Nothing but twiddle his thumbs.

S. If there were a railway from here to the moon, we could send the masters there, without a return ticket, and your weaving, your wife's spinning, your son's molding, would go on as before…Do you know what kind of profit was realized by your master last year?

W. We calculate that he must have got a hundred thousand francs.

S. How many workers does he employ; men, women and children, all included?

W. A hundred.

S. What wages do they get?

W. On average, about a thousand francs, also counting the salaries of managers and foremen.

S. So that the hundred workers in the work receive altogether a hundred thousand francs in wages, just enough to keep them from dying of hunger, while your master pocketed a hundred thousand francs for doing nothing. Where did these two hundred thousand francs come from?

W. Not from the sky; I have never seen it rain coins or bills.

S. It is the workers in his workshops and factories who have produced the hundred thousand francs they received in wages, and, besides, the hundred thousand francs profit of the master, who has used part of that for buying new machines.

W. There is no denying that.

S. Then it is the workers who produce the money which the master uses to buying new machines to make them work; it is the managers and foremen, wage slaves like yourself, who direct the production; where, then, does the master come in? What's he good for?

W. For exploiting labor.

S. Say rather, for robbing the laborer; that is clearer and more exact.

PERSONAL RECOLLECTIONS OF KARL MARX[1]

He was a man, take him for all in all,
I shall not look upon his like again.[2]

I MET KARL MARX FOR THE FIRST TIME IN FEBRUARY 1865. THE
First International had been founded on September 28, 1864, at
a meeting in St. Martin's Hall, London, and I went to London
from Paris to give Marx news of the development of the young
organization there. Mr. Tolain, now a senator in the bourgeois
republic and one of the representatives of the International at the
Berlin conference, gave me a letter of introduction.

I was then twenty-four years old. As long as I live I shall nor
forget the impression that first visit made on me. Marx was not
well at the time. He was working on the first book of *Capital*,
which was not published until two years later, in 1867. He feared
he would not be able to finish his work and was therefore glad
of visits from young people because, as he used to say, "I must
train those who will continue communist propaganda after me."

Karl Marx was one of the rare men who could be leaders in

1   ["Memories of K. Marx published by one of his closest collaborators, and
his son-in-law," first published in *Die Neue Zeit,* IX (1890–1891), 10–17; 37–42.
Die Neue Zeit ("The New Times" was a German socialist journal of the Social
Democratic Party of Germany published from 1883 to 1923. Translation by
Charles Kerr, modified by Ulrich Baer.)]
2   [Shakespeare, *Hamlet,* Act I, Sc. 2.]

science and public life at the same time: these two aspects were so closely linked in him that one can understand him only by taking into account both the scholar and the socialist fighter.

Marx held the view that science must be pursued for itself, without fear of whatever eventual results research could bring, but at the same time that a scientist could only debase himself by giving up active participation in public life or shutting himself up in his study or laboratory like a maggot in cheese without engaging in the life and social and political struggles of his contemporaries.

"Science must not be a selfish pleasure," Marx used to say. "Those who have the opportunity to be able to devote themselves to scientific research must be the first to place their knowledge at the service of humanity." One of his favorite sayings was: "Work for humanity."

Although Marx sympathised profoundly with the sufferings of the working classes, it was not sentimental considerations but the study of history and political economy that led him to communist views. He maintained that any unbiased man, free from the influence of private interests and not blinded by class prejudices, must necessarily come to the same conclusions.

Yet while studying the economic and political development of human society without any preconceived notions, Marx wrote with no other intention than to propagate the results of his research and with a determined will to provide a scientific basis for the socialist movement, which had so far been lost in the clouds of utopianism. He publicized his views only to aid in the triumph of the working class, whose historic mission is to establish communism as soon as it has achieved political and economic leadership of society...

Marx did not confine his activity to the country he was born in. "I am a citizen of the world," he used to say; "I am active wherever I am." And in fact, no matter what country events and political persecution drove him to France, Belgium, England—he took a prominent part in the revolutionary movements which developed there.

However, it was not the untiring and incomparable socialist agitator but rather the scientist that I first saw in his study in Maitland Park Road. That study was the center to which comrades came from all parts of the civilized world to debate with the master of socialist thought. One must know that historic room before one can begin to enter into the depths of Marx's spiritual life.

The study was on the first floor, flooded by light from a broad window that looked out on to the park. Opposite the window and on either side of the fireplace the walls were lined with bookcases filled with books and stacked up to the ceiling with newspapers and manuscripts. Opposite the fireplace on one side of the window were two tables piled up with papers, books, and newspapers; in the middle of the room, in a well-lit spot, stood a small, very simple desk (three foot by two) and a wooden armchair; between the armchair and the bookcases, opposite the window, was a leather sofa on which Marx used to lie down for a rest from time to time. On the mantelpiece were more books, cigars, matches, tobacco boxes, paperweights, and photographs of Marx's daughters and wife, and of Wilhelm Wolff and Frederick Engels.

Marx was a heavy smoker. "*Capital*," he said to me once, "will not even pay for the cigars I smoked writing it." But he was still heavier on matches. He so often forgot his pipe or cigar that he emptied an incredible number of boxes of matches in a short time to relight them.

He never allowed anybody to put his books or papers in order—or rather in disorder. The disorder in which they lay only looked that way: everything was really in its intended place so that it was easy for him to locate the book or notebook he needed. Even during conversations he often paused to show in the book a quotation or figure he had just mentioned. He and his study were one: the books and papers in it were as much under his control as his own limbs.

Marx had no use for formal symmetry in the arrangement of his books: volumes of different sizes and pamphlets stood next to one another. He arranged them according to their contents, not their size. Books were tools for his mind, not articles of luxury. "They are my slaves and they must serve me as I will," he used to say. He paid no heed to size or binding, quality of paper or type; he would turn down the corners of the pages, make pencil marks in the margin and underline whole lines. He never wrote anything in a book, but sometimes he could not refrain from an exclamation or question mark when the author went too far. His system of underlining made it easy for him to find any passage he needed in any book. He had the habit of going through his notebooks and reading the passages underlined in the books after intervals of many years in order to keep them fresh in his memory. He had an extraordinarily reliable memory which he had cultivated from his youth according to Hegel's advice by learning by heart verse in a foreign language he did not know.

He knew Heine and Goethe by heart and often quoted them in his conversations; he was an assiduous reader of poets in all European languages. Every year he reread Aeschylus in the Greek original. He considered him and Shakespeare as the greatest dramatic geniuses humanity ever produced. His respect for Shakespeare was boundless: he made a detailed study of his works and knew even the least important of all of his characters. His whole family maintained a veritable cult for the great English dramatist; his three daughters knew many of his works by heart. When after 1848 he wanted to perfect his knowledge of English, which he could already read, he sought out and classified all of Shakespeare's original expressions. He did the same with part of the polemical works of William Cobbett, of whom he had a high opinion. Dante and Robert Burns ranked among his favorite poets and he would listen with great pleasure to his daughters reciting or singing the Scottish poet's satires or love ballads.

Cuvier, an untirable worker and one of the great scientific minds, had a suite of rooms, arranged for his personal use, in the Paris Museum, of which he was director. Each room was intended for a particular pursuit and contained the books, instruments, anatomic aids, etc., required for the purpose. When he felt tired of one kind of work he would go into the next room and engage in another; this simple change of mental occupation, it is said, was a rest for him.

Marx was just as tireless a worker as Cuvier, but he had not the means to fit out several studies. He would rest by pacing up and down the room. A strip was worn out on the carpet from the door to the window, as sharply defined as a track across a meadow.

From time to time he would lie down on the sofa and read a novel; he sometimes read two or three at a time, alternating one with another. Like Darwin, he was a great reader of novels, his preference being for those of the eighteenth century, particularly Fielding's *Tom Jones.* The more modern novelists whom he found most interesting were Paul de Kock, Charles Lever, Alexandre Dumas (also known as Alexandre Dumas père) and Walter Scott, whose *Old Mortality* he considered a masterpiece. He had a definite preference for tales of adventure and humorous stories.

He ranked Cervantes and Balzac above all other novelists. In *Don Quixote* he saw the epic of dying-out chivalry whose virtues were ridiculed and scoffed at in the emerging bourgeois world. He admired Balzac so much that he wished to write a review of his great work *La Comédie Humaine* as soon as he had finished his book on economics. He considered Balzac not only as the historian of his time, but as the prophetic creator of characters which were still in their embryonic stages in the days of Louis Philippe and did not fully develop until Napoleon III (1848), after the author's death. Marx could read all European languages and write in three: German, French, and English, to the astonishment of anyone fluent in them. He liked to repeat the saying: "A foreign language is a weapon in the struggles of life."

He had a great talent for languages which his daughters inherited from him. He took up the study of Russian when he was already fifty years old, and although that language had no close affinity to any of the modern or ancient languages he knew, in six months he knew it well enough to derive pleasure from reading Russian poets and prose writers, his preference going to Pushkin, Gogol, and Saltykov-Shchedrin. He studied Russian in order to be able to read the documents of official inquiries which were redacted and suppressed by the Russian Government because the Czar feared the terrible revelations they contained. Devoted friends sent the documents to Marx and he was certainly the only political economist in Western Europe who had knowledge of them.

Besides the poets and novelists, Marx had another remarkable way of relaxing intellectually—mathematics, for which he had a special affinity. Algebra even brought him moral consolation and he took refuge in the most distressing moments of his eventful life. During his wife's last illness he was unable to devote himself to his usual scientific work and the only way in which he could shake off the oppression caused by her sufferings was to plunge into mathematics. During that time of moral suffering he wrote a work on infinitesimal calculus which, according to the opinion of experts, is of great scientific value. He saw in higher mathematics the most logical and at the same time the simplest form of dialectical movement. He held the view that science is not really developed until it has learned to make use of mathematics.

Although Marx's library contained over a thousand volumes carefully collected during his lifelong research work, it was not enough for him, and for years he regularly attended the British Museum, whose catalogue he appreciated very highly.

Even Marx's opponents were forced to acknowledge his extensive and profound erudition, not only in his own specialty—political economy—but in history, philosophy, and the literature of all countries.

In spite of the late hour at which Marx went to bed he was always up between eight and nine in the morning, had some black coffee, read through his newspapers and then went to his study, where he worked till two or three in the morning. He interrupted his work only for meals and, when the weather allowed, for a walk on Hampstead Heath in the evening. During the day he sometimes slept for an hour or two on the sofa. In his youth he often worked the whole night through.

Marx had a passion for work. He was so absorbed in it that he often forgot his meals. He had often to be called several times before he came down to the dining-room and hardly had eaten the last mouthful when he was back in his study.

He was a very light eater and even suffered from lack of appetite. This he tried to overcome by highly flavored food—ham, smoked fish, caviar, pickles; his stomach had to suffer greatly for the enormous activity of his brain.

He sacrificed his whole body to his brain; thinking was his greatest enjoyment. I often heard him repeat the words of Hegel, the master philosopher of his youth: "Even the criminal thought of a lawbreaker has more grandeur and nobility than all the wonders of heaven."

His physical constitution had to be good to put up with this unusual way of life and exhausting mental work. He was, in fact, of powerful build, more than average height, broad-shouldered, deep-chested, and had well-proportioned limbs, although the spinal column was rather long in comparison with the legs, as is often the case with Jews. Had he done gymnastics in his youth he would have become a very strong man. The only physical exercise he ever pursued regularly was walking: he could ramble or climb hills for hours, chatting and smoking, and not feel at all tired. One can say that he even worked walking in his room, only sitting down for short periods to write what he thought out while walking. He liked to walk up and down while talking, stopping from time to time when the explanation became more animated or the conversation serious.

For many years I went with him on his evening walks on Hampstead Heath and it was while strolling over the meadows with him that I got my education in economics. Without noticing it he expounded to me the whole contents of the first book of *Capital* as he was in the process of writing it.

On my return home I always wrote down as well as I could all I had heard. At first it was difficult for me to follow Marx's profound and complicated reasoning. Unfortunately I have lost those precious notes, for after the Commune the police ransacked and burned my papers in Paris and Bordeaux.

What I regret most is the loss of the notes I took on the evening when Marx, with the abundance of proof and considerations which was typical of him, expounded his brilliant theory of the development of human society. It was as if scales fell from my eyes. For the first time I saw clearly the logic of world history and could trace the apparently so contradictory phenomena of the development of society and human thought to their material origins. I felt dazzled, and the impression remained for years.

The Madrid socialists had the same impression when I developed to them as well as my feeble powers would allow that most magnificent of Marx's theories, which is beyond doubt one of the greatest ever elaborated by the human brain.

Marx's brain was armed with an unbelievable stock of facts from history, natural science, and philosophical theories. He was remarkably skilled in making use of the knowledge and observations accumulated during years of intellectual work. You could question him at any time on any subject and get the most detailed answer you could wish for, always accompanied by philosophical reflections of general application. His brain was like a man-of-war in port under steam, ready to launch into any direction in the ocean of thought.

There is no doubt that *Capital* reveals to us a mind of astonishing vigor and superior knowledge. But for me, as for all those who knew Marx intimately, neither *Capital* nor any other of his works shows all the magnitude of his genius or the extent of his knowledge. As a person, he was in fact superior to his works.

I worked with Marx; I was only the scribe to whom he dictated, but that gave me the opportunity of observing his manner of thinking and writing. Work was easy for him, and at the same time difficult. Easy because his mind found no difficulty in embracing the relevant facts and considerations in their completeness. But that very completeness made the exposition of his ideas a matter of long and arduous work.

Vico said: "The thing is only a vessel for God who knows everything; for humans who see nothing but the exterior, it is nothing but a surface."

Marx grasped things in the manner of Vico's god: He saw not only the surface, but could penetrate it by examining all the constituent parts in their mutual action and reaction; he isolated each of those parts and traced the history of the object's development. Then he went on from the thing to its surroundings and observed the reaction of one upon the other. He traced the origin of the object, the changes, evolutions, and revolutions it went through, and proceeded finally to its remotest effects. He did not see a thing in isolation, in itself and for itself, separate from its surroundings: he saw a highly complicated world in continual motion.

His intention was to disclose the whole of that world in its manifold and continually varying action and reaction. Men of letters of Flaubert's and the Goncourts' school complain that it is so difficult to render exactly what one sees; yet all they wish to render is the surface, the impression that they get. Their literary work is child's play in comparison with Marx's: it required extraordinary vigor of thought to grasp reality and render what he saw and wanted to make others see.

Marx was never satisfied with his work—he was always making some improvements and he always found his expressions inferior to the idea he wished to convey…

Marx had the two qualities of a genius mind: he had an incomparable talent for dissecting a thing into its constituent parts, and he was equally masterful at reconstituting the dissected object from these parts, with all their different forms of development, and discovering their mutual inner relations. His conclusions were not abstractions—which was the reproach made to him by economists who were themselves incapable of thinking. His method was not that of the geometrician who takes his definitions from the world around him but completely disregards reality in drawing his conclusions. You will not find a specific definition or isolated formula in *Capital* but a series of the most searching analyses which bring out the most subtle nuances and the finest gradations.

Marx begins by stating the plain fact that the wealth of a society dominated by the capitalist mode of production presents itself as an enormous accumulation of commodities. The commodity—a concrete object, not a mathematical abstraction—is therefore the element, the cell, of capitalist wealth. Marx now seizes on the commodity, turns it over and over and inside out, and pries out of it one secret after another that official economists were not in the least aware of, although those secrets are more numerous and profound than all the mysteries of the Catholic religion. Having examined the commodity in all its aspects, he considers it in its relations to its fellow commodity in the mode of exchange. Then he goes on to its production and the historic conditions necessary for its production. He considers the different forms which commodities assume and shows how they pass from one to another, how one form necessarily produces the other. He expounds the logical course of development of phenomena with such perfect artistry that one could think he had imagined it. And yet it has been taken from reality and is the expression of the actual dialectics of the commodity.

Marx was always extremely conscientious in his work. He never gave a fact or figure that was not borne out by the best authorities. He was never satisfied with secondhand information but always went to the source itself, no matter how tedious the process. To verify a minor fact he was wholly capable of running to the British Museum and consult its holdings. His critics were never able to prove that he was negligent or that he based his arguments on facts which did not bear strict checking.

His habit of always going to the very source made him read authors who were very little known and whom he was the only one to quote. *Capital* contains so many quotations from little-known authors that one might think Marx wanted to show off how well read he was. He had no intention of the sort. "I administer historical justice," he said. "I give each one his due." He considered himself obliged to name the author who had first expressed an idea or formulated it most correctly, no matter how insignificant and little known he was.

Marx was just as conscientious from the literary as from the scientific point of view. Not only would he never base himself on a fact he was not absolutely sure of, he never allowed himself to talk of a thing before he had studied it thoroughly. He did not publish a single work without repeatedly revising it until he had found the most appropriate form. He could not bear to appear in public without thorough preparation. It would have been a torture for him to show his manuscripts before giving them the finishing touch. He felt so strongly about this that he told me one day that he would rather burn his manuscripts than leave them unfinished.

His method of working often imposed upon him tasks the magnitude of which the reader can hardly imagine. Thus, in order to write the twenty pages or so on English legislation for labor protection in *Capital* he went through a whole library of *Blue Books* containing reports of commissions and factory inspectors in England and Scotland. He read them from cover to cover, as can be seen from the pencil marks in them. He considered those reports as the most important and weighty documents for the study of the capitalist mode of production. He had such a high opinion of those in charge of them that he doubted the possibility of finding in another country in Europe "men as competent, as free from partisanship and respect of persons as are the English factory inspectors." He paid them this brilliant tribute in the Preface to *Capital*.

From these *Blue Books* Marx drew a wealth of factual information. Many members of the British House of Commons and the House of Lords to whom they are distributed use them only as shooting targets, judging the striking power of the gun by the number of pages pierced. Others sell them by the pound, which is the most reasonable thing they can do, for this enabled Marx to buy them cheap from the old paper dealers in Long Acre whom he used to visit to look through their old books and papers. Professor Beesly said that Marx was the man who made the greatest use of English official inquiries and brought them to the knowledge of the world. He did not know that before

1845 Engels had already taken numerous documents from the *Blue Books* in writing his book on the condition of the working classes in England.

2.

TO GET TO KNOW AND LOVE THE HEART THAT BEAT WITHIN the breast of Marx the scholar you had to see him when he had closed his books and notebooks and was surrounded by his family, or on Sunday evenings in the company of his friends. He then proved the pleasantest, most inspiring, and funniest, with a laugh that came straight from the heart. His black eyes under the arches of his bushy brews sparkled with pleasure and irony whenever he heard a witty saying or a well-played repartee.

He was a loving, gentle, and indulgent father. "Children should educate their parents," he used to say. There was never even a trace of the authoritative parent in his relations with his daughters, whose love for him was extraordinary. He never gave them an order, but asked them to do what he wished as a favor or made them feel that they should not do what he wanted to forbid them. And yet a father could seldom have had more docile children than he. His daughters considered him as their friend and treated him as a companion; they did not call him "father", but "moor"—a nickname that he owed to his dark complexion and jet-black hair and beard. The members of the Communist League, on the other hand, called him "Father Marx" before 1848, when he was not even thirty years of age.

Marx used to spend hours playing with his children. They still remember the sea battles in a big basin of water and the burning of the fleets of paper ships that he made for them and set on fire to their great joy.

On Sundays his daughters would not allow him to work, he

belonged to them for the whole day. If the weather was fine, the whole family would go for a walk in the country. On their way they would stop at a modest inn for bread and cheese and ginger beer. When his daughters were still young he would make the long walk seem shorter to them by telling them endless fairy tales which he made up as he went, delaying or precipitating the complications according to the distance they had yet to go, so that the little ones forgot their weariness by listening.

He had an incomparably fertile imagination: his first literary works were poems. Mrs. Marx carefully preserved the poetry her husband wrote in his youth but never showed it to anybody. His family had dreamt of him being a man of letters or a university professor and thought he was debasing himself by engaging in socialist agitation and researching political economy, which was at that time hardly a respected discipline in Germany.

Marx had promised his daughters to write a drama on the Gracchi brothers for them.[3] Unfortunately he was unable to keep his word. It would have been interesting to see how he, who was called "the knight of the class struggle," would have dealt with that tragic and magnificent episode in the class struggle of the ancient world. Marx fostered a lot of plans which were never carried out. Among other works he intended to write a work of logic and a history of philosophy, the latter having been his favorite subject in his younger days. He would have needed to live to a hundred to carry out all his literary plans and present the world with a portion of the treasure hidden in his brain.

Marx's wife was his lifelong helpmate in the truest and fullest sense of the word. They had known each other as children and grown up together. Marx was only seventeen at the time of his engagement. Seven long years the young couple had to wait before they were married in 1843. After that they never parted.

3   [The brothers Tiberius Gracchus and Gaius Gracchus lived at the start of the late Roman Republic, and served in the plebeian tribunates of 133 BC and 122–121 BCE.]

Mrs. Marx died shortly before her husband. Nobody ever had a greater sense of equality than she, although she was born and raised in a German aristocratic family. No social differences or classifications existed for her. She entertained working people in their working clothes in her house and at her table with the same politeness and consideration as if they had been dukes or princes. A great number workers from all countries enjoyed her hospitality and I am convinced that not one of them ever dreamt that the woman who received them with such warm and sincere cordiality descended in the female line from the family of the Dukes of Argyll and that her brother was a minister of the King of Prussia…She had given up everything to follow her Karl and never, not even in times of dire need, was she sorry she had done so.

She had a clear and brilliant mind. Her letters to her friends, written without with ease and no apparent effort, are actual small masterpieces that testify to her lively and original thinking. It was a treat to get a letter from Mrs. Marx. Johann-Philipp Becker has published several of them. Heine, a pitiless satirist as he was, feared Marx's irony, but he was full of admiration for the penetrating sensitive mind of his wife. When the Marxes lived in Paris he was one of their regular visitors. Marx had such great respect for the intelligence and critical sense of his wife that he showed her all his manuscripts and set great store by her opinion, as he himself told me in 1866. Mrs. Marx copied out her husband's manuscripts before they were sent to the print-shop.

Mrs. Marx had a number of children. Three of them died at a tender age during the period of hardships that the family went through after the 1848 Revolution. At that time they had taken refugee in London in two small rooms in Dean Street, Soho Square. I only knew the three daughters. When I was introduced to Marx in 1865 his youngest daughter, now Mrs. Aveling, was a charming child with a boy's disposition. Marx used to say his wife had made a mistake as to sex when she brought her into the world. The other two daughters formed a most surprising and harmonious contrast. The eldest, Mrs. Longuet, had her father's dark and vigorous complexion, dark eyes, and jet-black hair. The second, Mrs. Lafargue, was fair-haired and rosy-skinned, and her rich curly hair had a golden shimmer as if it had caught the rays of the setting sun: she looked like her mother.

Another important member of the Marx household was Hélène Demuth. Born of a peasant family, she entered the service of Mrs. Marx long before the latter's wedding, when hardly more than a child. When her mistress got married she had not wanted to leave her and devoted herself with complete self-oblivion to the Marx family. She accompanied Mrs. Marx and her husband on all their journeys over Europe and even followed them into exile.

She was the benevolent spirit of the house and could always find a way out of the most difficult situations. It was thanks to her sense of order, her economy, and skill that the Marx family were never short of the bare essentials. There was nothing she could not do: she cooked, kept the house, dressed the children, cut clothes for them, and sewed them with Mrs. Marx. She was housekeeper and major domo at the same time: she ran the whole house. The children loved her like a mother and her maternal feeling towards them gave her a mother's authority. Mrs. Marx considered her as her bosom friend and Marx fostered a particular friendship towards her; he played chess with her, and often enough lost to her.

Helene loved the Marx family blindly: anything they did was good in her eyes and could not be otherwise; whoever criticized Marx had to deal with her. She extended her motherly protection to everyone who was admitted to intimacy with the Marxes. It was as though she had adopted all of the Marx family. She outlived Marx and his wife and transferred her care to Engels' household. She had known him since she was a girl and extended to him the attachment she had for the Marx family.

Engels was, so to speak, a member of the Marx family. Marx's daughters called him their second father. He was Marx's alter ego. For a long time the two names were never separated in Germany and they will be forever united in history. Marx and Engels were the personification in our time of the ideal friendship portrayed by the poets of antiquity. From their youth they developed together in parallel to each other, lived in intimate fellowship of ideas and feelings, and participated in the same revolutionary agitation; as long as they could stay together they worked in common.

Had events not parted them for about twenty years they would probably have worked together in this way their whole life. But after the defeat of the 1848 Revolution Engels had to go to Manchester, while Marx was obliged to remain in London. Even so, they continued their common intellectual life by writing to each other almost daily to share their views on the political and scientific events of the day, and to let the other see their work. As soon as Engels was able to free himself from his work he hurried from Manchester to London, where he set up his home only ten minutes away from his dear Marx. From 1870 to the death of his friend not a day went by without the two men seeing each other, sometimes at one's house, sometimes at the other's.

It was a day of rejoicing for the Marxes when Engels informed them that he was coming from Manchester. His pending visit was spoken of long beforehand, and on the day of his arrival Marx was so impatient that he could not work. The two friends spent the whole night smoking and drinking together and talking over all that had happened since their last meeting.

Marx appreciated Engels' opinion more than anybody else's, for Engels was a man he considered capable of being his collaborator. For him Engels was a whole audience. No effort could have

been too great for Marx to convince Engels and win him over to
his ideas. For instance, I have seen him read whole volumes over
and over to find the fact he needed to change Engels's opinion on
some secondary point that I do not remember concerning the
political and religious wars of the Albigenses. It was a triumph
for Marx to bring Engels round to his opinion.

Marx was proud of Engels. He took pleasure in enumerating
to me all of his friend's moral and intellectual qualities. He once
specially made the journey to Manchester with me to introduce
me to him. He admired the versatility of his knowledge and was
alarmed at the slightest thing that could befall him. "I always
tremble," he said to me, "for fear he should have an accident
during a hunt which he undertakes with such passion, gallop-
ing over the fields with slackened reins and not shying at any
obstacle."

Marx was as good a friend as he was a loving husband and
father. In his wife and daughters, Helene and Engels, he found
worthy objects of love for a man such as he was.

3.

HAVING STARTED AS ONE THE LEADERS OF THE RADICAL
bourgeoisie, Marx found himself deserted as soon as his opposition became too resolute and treated as an enemy as soon
as he became a communist. He was baited and expelled from
Germany after being insulted and defamed, and then there was
a conspiracy of silence against him and his work. *The Eighteenth
Brumaire*, which proves that Marx was the only historian and
politician of 1848 who understood and disclosed the real nature
of the causes and results of the coup d'état of December 2, 1851,
was completely ignored.[4] In spite of the timeliness of the work

---

4   [Marx wrote *The 18th Brumaire* between December 1851 and March

not a single bourgeois newspaper even mentioned it.

The Poverty of Philosophy, an answer to the *Philosophy of Poverty*, and *A Contribution to the Critique of Political Economy* (1859) were likewise ignored. But the First International and the first book of *Capital* broke this conspiracy of silence after it had lasted fifteen years. Marx could no longer he ignored. The International grew and filled the world with the glory of its achievements. Although Marx stayed in the background and let others act it was soon discovered who was the master mind behind the scenes.

The Social-Democratic Party was founded in Germany and became a power that Bismarck courted before he attacked it. Schweitzer, a follower of Lassalle, published a series of articles, which Marx highly praised, to bring *Capital* to the knowledge of the working public.[5] On a motion by Johann Philipp Becker the Congress of the International adopted a resolution directing the attention of socialists in all countries to *Capital* as to the "Bible of the working class."[6]

After the uprising on March 18, 1871, in which people tried to detect the work of the International, and after the defeat of the Commune, which the General Council of the First International took it upon itself to defend against the rage of the bourgeois press in all countries, Marx's name became famous the whole world. He was acknowledged as the greatest theoretician of scientific socialism and the organizer of the first international working-class movement. *Capital* became the manual of socialists in all countries. All socialist and working-class papers spread its theories. During a big strike which broke out in New York

---

1852; it was published in May 1852.]

5   [Jean Baptista von Schweitzer (1833–1875), German writer and politician; Ferdinand Lassalle (1825-1864), German-Prussian philosopher and political activist.]

6   [Jean-Philippe Becker (1809–1886), German revolutionary and editor, active in the International and friend of Marx's.]

extracts from *Capital* were disseminated in the form of leaflets to inspire the workers to resist and show them how justified their claims were.

Capital was translated into the main European languages—Russian, French, and English, and extracts were published in German, Italian, French, Spanish, and Dutch. Every time opponents in Europe or America made attempts to refute its theories, the economists immediately got a socialist reply which shut their mouths. *Capital* has truly become today what it was called by the Congress of the International—*the Bible of the working class.*

But Marx's active participation in the international socialist movement took time from his scientific research and writing. The death of his wife and that of his eldest daughter, Mrs. Longuet, also had an adverse effect on them.

Marx's love for his wife was profound and intimate. Her beauty had been his pride and his joy, her gentleness and devotedness had lightened for him the hardships necessarily resulting from his eventful life as a revolutionary socialist. The disease which led to the death of Mrs. Marx also shortened the life of her husband. During her long and painful illness Marx became exhausted in body and spirit by the loss of sleep, the emotional toll, and the lack of exercise and fresh air. He contracted the bronchitis which was to snatch him away.

On December 2, 1881, Mrs. Marx died as she had lived, a Communist and a materialist. Death had no terrors for her. When she felt her end approach she exclaimed: "Karl, my strength is ebbing." Those were her last intelligible words.

She was buried in Highgate Cemetery, in "unconsecrated ground," on December 5. Conforming to the habits of her life and Marx's, all care was taken to avoid her funeral being announced as a public one...Only a few close friends accompanied her to her last resting-place...Before leaving Engels delivered the eulogy over her grave.

After the death of his wife, Marx's life was a succession of physical and moral sufferings which he bore with great fortitude. They were aggravated by the sudden death of his eldest daughter, Mrs. Longuet, a year later. He was broken, never to recover.

He died at his desk on March 14, 1883, at the age of sixty-four.

BIOGRAPHICAL TIMELINE

1842   Paul Lafargue is born on January 15 in Santiago de
        Cuba, a city in Cuba that was then a Spanish colony, of
        Black African, Jewish, and Caribbean Native ancestry
        to a Creole mother and French Jewish father. He often
        stated that "the blood of three oppressed races ran in
        his veins," that he was an "internationalist of blood
        before he was one of ideology," and that he was "proud-
        est of [his] Negro extraction."

1848   The February Revolution occurs in France, leading to
        the establishment of the Second Republic.

1851   Louis-Napoleon Bonaparte stages a coup d'état and
        establishes himself as Emperor Napoleon III, usher-
        ing in the Second Empire. Lafargue's family moves to
        Bordeaux, France.

1860   Begins medical studies at Lyon.

1865   Continues studies in Paris and becomes involved in
        socialist circles.

1866   Barred from French universities for participating in
        student protests, continues studies in London.

1868   Becomes a member of the International Workingmen's
        Association (also known as the First International), an

organization founded by Karl Marx and others to promote the interests of the working class. Marries Marx's second-born daughter, Laura. Three children born in the following three years die in infancy.

1870　The Franco-Prussian War begins. Returns to France and fights on the side of the Paris Commune, a socialist and revolutionary government that briefly rules Paris in 1871.

1871　The Paris Commune is suppressed by the French government in May. Goes into exile in Spain until 1872.

1872　Moves to London and becomes a close associate of Marx and his family.

1875　Returns to France and becomes involved in socialist politics once again. Publishes "The Economic Materialism of Karl Marx," a study of Marxist economic theory.

1880　Publishes first of several versions of *The Right to Laziness* in installments in *L'Égalité*.

1881　Publishes "Socialism and Social Science," a critique of the prevailing bourgeois social theories of the time.

1882　Returns to France and helps found a Marxist party, the *Parti Ouvrier* (Worker's Party; "POF"). Works as editor of *L'Égalité*.

1883　Publishes "Socialism and Darwinism," in *Progress*, London.

1884　Gives public lectures on "The Economic Materialism of Karl Marx" in Paris.

1885　Arrested and imprisoned for refusal to pay a fine imposed earlier. Writes a critical essay on novelist

Victor Hugo. Laura Lafargue's French translation of the *Communist Manifesto* appears in installments in *L'Egalité*. Publishes a study of the materialist origins of goodness and justice in *La Revue philosophique.*

1890   Publishes "The Economic Evolution of the Nineteenth Century," a study of the economic and social changes over the previous century, as well as essays on Rousseau, the family, and (under the pseudonym "Fergus") public property. Speaks to demonstrating workers in London.

1891   Sentenced to a year in prison for his involvement in a protest against a military parade in Lille.

1892   Elected to the Chamber of Deputies as a delegate of the *Parti Ouvrier*, the first Marxist deputy, and the first person of African descent in France known to hold such an elected position.

1893   Writes essays on Marx's economic materialism, the French language before and after the Revolution, the role of myths, and other topics for *The New Era*, a French Marxist journal that also disseminates Engels' and Marx's writing in French translation.

1894   Loses seat in Parliament; attends *Parti Ouvrier* congress in Paris and retreats from direct political work. Publishes an essay on the "myth of Adam and Even" in *La Revue socialiste.*

1895   Publishes "Historical Materialism," a summary of Marxist theory. Meets Lenin in Paris. Delivers eulogy for Friedrich Engels, who was an important source of financial, intellectual and moral support. Denounces colonialism at the *Parti Ouvrier* congress.

1896   With money inherited from Engels' estate, the

Lafargues purchase a home in the Paris suburbs. Writes essays on a range of topics, including literature, history, mythology, philosophy, linguistics, religion, and economics; publishes defenses of Marxism against various critics. Attends the Second International's Congress in London as part of the French delegation.

1897   Publishes an essay on the theory of surplus value that defends Marx and results in critics of his work as unduly deferential.

1898   Withdraws from candidacy for a seat on the Municipal Council in Paris.

1899   Participates in debates about the nature of socialism at meetings of the *Parti Ouvrier*.

1900   Publishes "Socialism and the Intellectuals" in pamphlet from.

1901   Participates in the *Parti Ouvrier's* regional congress.

1904   Publishes a pamphlet titled "The Woman Question" and a critical article on "Christian Charity."

1905   Publishes essay on belief in God.

1906   Publishes articles on "Patriotism and the Bourgeoisie."

1910   Lenin visits the Lafargues in their home in Draveil.

1911   Travels to Italy and Southern France with his wife, Laura. On November 26, with his wife, commits what in a note he calls "rational suicide" in their home in Draveil, France. Lenin gives a eulogy; the Lafargues are buried in the Cimetière du Père-Lachaise in Paris.

www.ingramcontent.com/pod-product-compliance
Lightning Source LLC
Chambersburg PA
CBHW032117280326
41933CB00009B/876